The Short Book

The Short Book

Tall Stories, Freakish Facts, & the Long &
Short of Being Small in a Great Big World

Written and Illustrated by

Zachary Kanin

BLACK DOG
& LEVENTHAL
PUBLISHERS
NEW YORK

ISBN-13: 978-1-57912-751-0

Library of Congress Cataloging-in-Publication Data

Kanin, Zachary.
  The short book / by Zachary Kanin.
       p. cm.
  Includes bibliographical references and index.
  ISBN 978-1-57912-751-0
  1. Stature, Short. I. Title.

  QP84.K36 2007
  612.6'6—dc22

                                        2007024164

Book design: Cindy LaBreacht

Manufactured in the USA

Published by
Black Dog & Leventhal Publishers, Inc.
151 West 19th Street
New York, New York 10011

Distributed by
Workman Publishing Company
225 Varick Street
New York, New York 10014

Photo credits: page 18: La Donna Hudson; page 21: Richard Carson/ Reuters/Corbis; page 35: Collection of James G. Mundie; page 50: AP Images; page 165: Collection of the author.

g f e d c b a

This book is dedicated to my brothers, Jonah and Frank, who, though of various heights, are both of a lesser age than myself, and I thank them for that.

ACKNOWLEDGMENTS

I acknowledge first and foremost my parents, Carol and Dennis, who gave me the strength to finish this incredible achievement.

Second, my research assistant and girlfriend, Christina Angelides, who was always there for me, even when I was hospitalized for excessive complaining.

My editor, Laura Ross, who was an incredible editor who believed in me from the very middle.

Robert Mankoff, my former boss and mentor, for encouraging me to take night classes and get my G.E.D.

Josh Lambert, Karen Bidgood, Stephen and Susan Polis Schutz, and all the people at Blue Mountain Press, for giving me the opportunity to write this book in the first place.

J.P. Leventhal, True Sims, Marie Mundaca, and all the people at Black Dog & Leventhal, for giving me the opportunity to write this book in the second place.

Cindy LaBreacht and Iris Bass, for making sure things were correct and readable and otherwise breezy and free.

Professor Stephen Greenblatt, for kindly answering my one e-mail.

Professors Cecil MacKinnon and Hovey Burgess, for a day of circus history and hamburgers I will never forget.

Asha Schecter and Katherine Furman, for helping to find the photos when no one else would.

Sarah Larson, Matt Podolsky, Doe Coover, and Jenny Volvovski for telling me if I was right or wrong about my thoughts on different occasions.

Simon Rich and Matt Diffee, for thanking me in their books.

And finally, my grandparents, for writing this book.

Contents

Foreword
Why Read the Short Book? **11**

PART ONE Shortspective **15**
Everything has its price. The price of shortness
is reading this chapter about size comparisons.

PART TWO Smallotry **45**
Uh-oh, some people are mean to those
blessed with shortness.

PART THREE Profiles in Shortage **85**
Get ready to be shocked by who is short.

PART FOUR Suppshort **131**
Finally, we get to the good stuff: heavy-handed advice.

A Neat Little Package **171**
The end of the book.

Foreword

If you're like me, you're short. That's something you deal with every day, and sometimes at night. Believe it or not, almost 80 percent of the world's population considers themselves short—which means that about 30 percent of short people are actually taller than average! Is that an accurate statistic? I hope so.

Which brings us to an important point. I am not a scientist. You'll be reminded of that fact a lot in this book, and it will always be true, but there may be some points where you start to forget I am not a scientist and then BOOM, you remember. I'm just giving you fair warning. This is not a textbook. If it were, it would cost a lot more money and you would be taking the weirdest class in the world.

I am not a scientist, but this book is full of facts that will blow your mind. Being short is no laughing matter. It is a very serious occupation that even the greatest emperors in the world have taken on full time: Alexander the Great conquered the world wearing a child's set of armor, Napoleon Bonaparte had to stand on tippy-toes to be crowned emperor, and the musician Prince grooves at five foot two.

Being short is tough. But it's also fun. And strange. And exciting! It is sometimes thoughtful, occasionally interesting, and once in a blue moon it is languid. Many of the most important and famous people in the world were short, and none of them could get a date to the prom. Maybe after reading this book, you'll be able to get a date more easily. I don't know. The two events wouldn't be related, but I just have a really good feeling about you.

So, why should you read this book? For one thing, it might make you feel better about being short. Most people have no idea that Picasso, Beethoven, Kant, Voltaire, and Mother Teresa were all short. And that is only the tip of the iceberg.

So sit back in your high chair, toss back a few tall-boys, kick off your ten-inch heels, and enjoy. Being short has never had it so tall.

What You'll Find In This Book

★ A lot of chapters
★ Some facts
★ Some white lies
★ One horrible secret
★ Pictures of animals
★ One actual animal
★ The reason you are short
★ Some other people who are short
★ My Social Security number
★ Your name (provided you have the same name as me)
★ Keys to a special locket that is hidden somewhere in your kitchen
★ Instructions on how to destroy the contents of that evil locket
★ Average heights in different countries
★ The short person's national anthem
★ Tax forms
★ A receipt for this book placed between the pages by the cashier
★ The cashier's phone number
★ A big lipstick smear by the cashier
★ A maze with two solutions and no survivors
★ More facts
★ A ton more lies

You Will Not Find
Big Foot

Testimonials

"Whenever I go to the bank, I am handed a lollipop instead of a deposit slip. When will the discrimination end? And if the answer is 'soon,' then where can I buy these lollipops once they stop becoming available through the bank? Please tell me the answer to my questions in your book."—MARY TOMAS

"I am a general in the army, but I am also pretty tall. If I wanted to utilize the Napoleonic Complex would it be reasonable to just ride a really short horse? I think that would probably make me insecure enough, but really, only a book would be able to tell me for sure. Scientifically, that is."—GEN. ARMAND T. OMAS

"Every morning I wake up and I've fallen out of bed. I think one side of my bed is lower than the other. It would really help if I had a small book to place under that side so my bed would be more level. Actually, now that I think about it, that would be really important."
—TOMAS KINCAID

"This book really makes me think twice about military spending."
—GEN. ALAN CORNING

"If global warming is the single greatest threat to our national security, then this book is number two."—EDWIN ROGERS (a scientist)

"Is dieting really responsible for more deaths than all of the world's wars and diseases combined? I have to believe that it is, because it is in this book."—TOM A. S.

"Before I read this book I was short—now I'm tall. You do the math."
—TOMAS

"*The Short Book* is the first book I've read in a long time without stopping for food or water or air."—(The Late) TOM SASCA

"Do you have a lot of money? If so, buy this book. If not, buy food and whatever insurance you can afford."—ZACHARY KANIN

"I work with a lot of short people and this book helped me to realize that they are people, not just tiny furniture."—MICHAEL JORDACHE

"I'm a big, important businessman, and I don't have time to read a lot of books, so, yeah, I never read this book."—FLORIO CHAMBERS

"I'm waiting for the movie."—EDNA

"I heard Zach Kanin is unstable."—SUSAN

"I heard Zach Kanin is a Communist sympathizer."—HAROLD

"Well I heard he voted for Nader."—ROBERT

"He didn't!"—EDNA

"I swear, I have it on good authority he voted for Nader in 2000."
—ROBERT

"What an idiot."—EDNA

"I know."—ROBERT

PART ONE

Shortspective

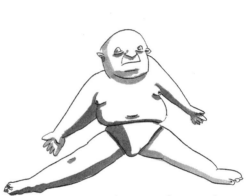

IMPORTANT: Make sure you're short and not just standing with your legs really far apart.

Why Am I So Short?

I was born with an adult head and a tiny body.
Like a *Peanuts* character.—JON STEWART

THE SCIENCE BEHIND THE HEIGHT

When I was about thirteen, my family doctor shattered my dreams of being 5'10" like my old man. He said I was only going to be 5'8". I was devastated. How could this have happened? Now I would never be able to slam-dunk a basketball or be the world's tallest man.

As upsetting as this news seemed, by my next annual checkup I hadn't grown a single centimeter. It appeared that I was stuck at 5'3"! I was done growing.

Doctors probed my hips and fondled my shins to find out why I had stopped growing. Every part of me was measured and remeasured. My hands, feet, and limbs were all X-rayed; extensive family histories were delved into; and finally a diagnosis was reached: I'm short.

BUT WHY?

As I learned, the most important factor in determining your final height is

(drumroll)...

Your Parents Hate You

The primary reason you are the height you are is genetics. That means that however tall your parents are, that's pretty much how tall you're going to be. And that means that your parents basically decide how tall you're gonna be, and you're not tall, so they hate you. And I'm not tall, so I love you. You dig?

TWO CRAPPY FACTS

★ It is difficult to know exactly which genes control height because some studies show that as few as seven to as many as twenty genes contribute to a person's growth. It's difficult to know, but I do know. I'm just not telling.

★ The study of height is called auxology. The study of bartending is called mixology. A mixolauxologist is a made-up word that a drunk person cannot say correctly.

But it's not ALL about genetics. Based on my parent's height charts, I *should* have grown to 5'10", but did not. Thus, in my case, genetics did not immediately answer the question, Why was I short? What else could it have been?

YOUR PARENTS ABUSED YOU IN MORE WAYS THAN YOU CAN KNOW

Another cause of shortness is... **growth failure**. ☹ Failure? I didn't even know I was being *graded*! Seriously though, failure to grow to your full genetic potential can happen for any of the following reasons:

POOR NUTRITION: For their bodies to grow, children need to not only eat a lot of healthy food, but also get plenty of exercise and sleep. Ideally, parents should make their kids sleep on treadmills and nap with two medicine balls taped to their chests.

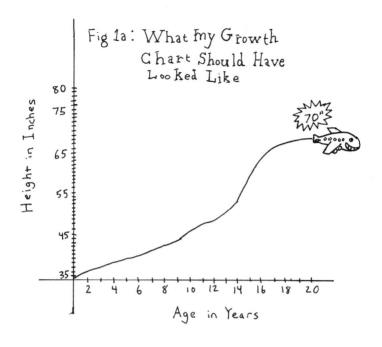

Fig 1a: What My Growth Chart Should Have Looked Like

Height in Inches

80
75
65
55
45
35

70"

2 4 6 8 10 12 14 16 18 20

Age in Years

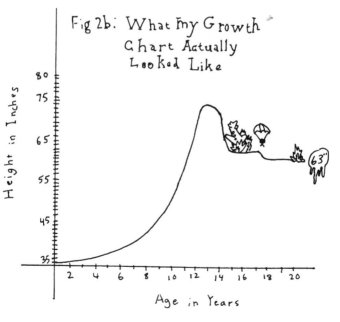

Fig 2b: What My Growth Chart Actually Looked Like

Height in Inches

80
75
65
55
45
35

63"

2 4 6 8 10 12 14 16 18 20

Age in Years

ILLNESS: Many diseases that occur before birth or during childhood can cause growth failure. For a list of these diseases, enroll in medical school.

STRESS AND PHYSICAL ABUSE: Some studies suggest that child abuse or too much fighting in a household can stunt a child's growth. No word yet on the effects of not enough fighting.

ENDOCRINE FAILURE: Some people don't grow because their bodies don't produce enough growth hormone. In a case like this, a person can get growth hormone treatments, which we will discuss in Part 4. I would discuss it now, but your dad promised me he'd play catch with me and take me to get ice cream, at a strip club.

DWARFISM is shortness due to an underdevelopment of the body. There are 320 different types of dwarfism and it affects over 1.5 million people in the United States alone. The most common form of dwarfism is achondroplasia, which affects the bones and results in a body with a normal torso, a large head, and small arms and legs. Do I, personally, blame your parents for this? You better believe it.

A cause of less severe shortness is **CONSTITUTIONAL GROWTH DELAY (CGD).** CGD is a condition in which a person develops later than his or her peers. On the other end of the spectrum is **PRECOCIOUS PUBERTY,** which is when you hit puberty too early, so your body finishes growing before you get all your inches. I had my growth spurt when I was eleven. Big mistake. While I was awesomely using deodorant and buying a larger pair of sweatpants, other kids were saving up their bones and skin for bigger bodies.

But what if none of these factors explains your height? What if you're just short for no reason?

I CAN'T MAKE THIS ANY MORE CLEAR: YOUR PARENTS WOULD RATHER PAY BILLS IN HELL THAN SEE YOU HAPPY!

If you're short for no discernible reason, that is called **IDIOPATHIC SHORT STATURE.** Although it's hard to blame this directly on your parents, remember that while you were still struggling to exist, they were having unprotected sex all over the place. And that's enough to make anyone resentful.

WHAT YOU WOULD LOOK LIKE IF YOUR PARENTS LOVED YOU

Fig. 1C: A well-adjusted human being.

So, why was *I* short? Here are a few guesses: First, I only ate spare ribs and gingerbread cake. Second, I went through puberty at eleven. Lastly, I may have had intrauterine growth retardation—a congenital illness. So...the mix of poor nutrition, precocious puberty, a congenital illness (and some idiopathic shortness for good measure) may all have contributed. Luckily, being short is the best thing that ever happened to me; if I were tall, I wouldn't be able to write this book! (I'm writing on a computer that's very close to the ground.)

An Alternative History of Why I Am So Short

Free will and fate alike have been kind to me. First, my parents decided to have a kid and then fate decided to make me short. But it's not only chance that makes a person short; there are other factors as well:

★ Sunshine
★ God's divine intervention
★ Too much love from friends and family
★ A rainbow made of candy hearts on the day you were born
★ You're a genius
★ You accidentally died and went to heaven
★ Heaven actually came down to earth, but just for the span when you were going through puberty
★ The soil around your house is made of magic
★ Someone used his third wish to make you short
★ You're not short, your body is just made of thousands of pounds of gold so you sink into the ground when you walk
★ Genetics

Yup. There are a lot of plausible, scientific reasons why you and I turned out so good, and wait! Here is one more:

★ You are wonderful.

Am I Too Tall to Read This Book?

Are you worried that you're not short? Here's some advice: stop worrying so much—it is bad for your veins. And why should you worry, when even people who are 5'11" often give their height as 6', and most people, even the ones you think of as "average height," exaggerate their height because they think they should be taller.

HOW SHORT IS SHORT?

Shortness is comparative. When Eve popped out of Adam's rib cage, his first words were, "What are those?" pointing to her breasts. His second words were, "Now that there is another person, I know that I am tall and you, Eve, are short; I am fat and you are thin; and we are in deep, deep love." He never stopped pointing at her breasts, which sort of ruined the moment, but you get the picture: someone can only be tall or short compared with someone else.

Most people judge whether they are short or tall by looking at the people nearby. The mean height in America for an adult male is 5'9" and for an adult female it is 5'4½". But if you live in a different country or if you live a hundred years in the past, then the average height of the people around you is probably completely different.

DIFFERENT REGIONS OF THE WORLD HAVE DIFFERENT HEIGHTS

Height within a population is determined primarily by genetics, whereas nutrition and environment determine whether a whole population is taller or shorter than another. Thus, places where better nutrition and medicine are available will have taller populations.

....

TRY THESE OUT FOR SIZE

If you were a 5'9" male among the Efe and Basua tribes, you would be a giant—they are the shortest people in the world, averaging 4'9" for men and 4'6" for women.

If you were a 5'9" male in the Dinka Nilotles tribe in Southern Sudan, hoo boy, would you be small! They're the tallest, averaging 6' for men and 5'6" for women.

....

Weather also plays a role, because shorter people with shorter limbs require less energy so they can maintain heat better. That is why Eskimos are generally shorter than people who live in warm climates.

This is another reason:

SOME AVERAGE HEIGHTS FROM AROUND THE GLOBE

	MEN	WOMEN
Australia	5'10"	5'4.6"
Austria	5'10.9"	5'4.9"
Brazil	5'6.9"	5'1.1"
Canada	5'10.9"	5'4.9"
China	5'6"	5'2"
France	5'8.2"	5'3.7"
Vietnam	5'3"	4'10"
The Netherlands	6'1"	5'8"

Disclaimer: Not all of these averages are exact. Accurate average heights are almost impossible to come by, and even when data is available, people can lie about their height. Another thing to remember is that I am not a scientist.

» 24 «

Vietnam is presently one of the shortest nations because of famine and turmoil in the region. The Dutch are the tallest people in the world and growing—taller and fatter; half of their population is now overweight.

DIFFERENT GENDERS HAVE DIFFERENT HEIGHTS

Ladies and Gentlemen. They sound so similar, but they are so different. On average, women are thirteen centimeters shorter than men.

Because for most of history only men could join the military, and because our most accurate height records from the past are from military enlistments, we have very few historical female heights. The other reason is that "a lady never reveals her height."

SPEAKING OF THE MILITARY...

While the age restrictions to enlist in the North Korean army have stayed the same, the height requirements have dropped from 4'11" to 4'2", because of nationwide stunted growth due to famine. I'm only telling you this because it seems like it would be a pretty laid-back, chill army to join, if you are interested.

DIFFERENT RACES HAVE DIFFERENT HEIGHTS

The average white male and the average black male in the United States are taller than men of other racial groups. Black women are taller than the women of most other racial groups in the United States. What does all this say about racial harmony? Nothing, I guess.

WE ARE DIFFERENT HEIGHTS AT DIFFERENT TIMES OF THE DAY

Get the hell out of here. It's true! Over the course of the day we shrink between ¾ inch and 1½ inches due to the pressure of gravity on our bodies. We stretch back out when we sleep at night. Many celebrities have their pictures taken early in the morning, so they can look their tallest. Many normal people have their pictures taken in the shower, by the government.

Historical Heights

Tell a group of people that Beethoven was only five foot four and they'll say, "What? Really? Well, people were much shorter back then." People always think that "people were much shorter back then," and they are often correct. However, it is not as simple as a steady evolution toward a more ideal, taller height.

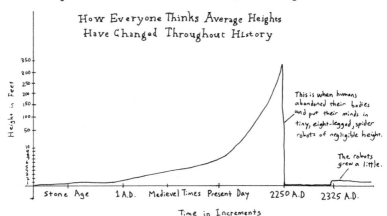

How Everyone Thinks Average Heights Have Changed Throughout History

This is when humans abandoned their bodies and put their minds in tiny, eight-legged, spider robots of negligible height.

The robots grew a little.

THE FIRST HUMANS

It is debatable which primitive species of humans is directly related to us, but by studying fossils of many different hominids, we learn that the earliest humans weren't so much shorter than we are. However, they were much, much funnier. Here is one of their jokes:

CAVEMAN 1: Knock, knock.
CAVEMAN 2: Run, we are under attack by the men with knocking clubs!

Homo Erectus   Homo Sapiens

THE MIDDLE AGES TO THE PRESENT

When Charlemagne conquered England a thousand years ago, he stood six feet above sea level and was often mistaken for one of the pillars of Stonehenge. Seven centuries later, the Frenchman storming the Bastille averaged a mere five feet in height and one hundred pounds, and were often mistaken for delicious, buttered baguettes.

THE INDUSTRIAL REVOLUTION

Heights have not changed so much since the Stone Age, but in the last two centuries the world has been growing. The Industrial Revolution of the eighteenth century was an exception: people shrank. Long, sedentary hours and rising costs of food made people stinky and unhealthy, and thus short (the stinkier you are, the shorter you are—that's just common sense).

> **ANTHROPOMETRY**
>
> By looking at height changes in populations, anthropometrists can figure out key economic and environmental factors about different time periods. For instance, the fact that the French were shorter around the time of the French Revolution suggests that they had less money, which explains why so few jet skis were sold in France during those years. That is one more mystery solved, thanks to pseudoscience.

THE PLAINS INDIANS

In the mid-nineteenth century, the tallest people in the world were North America's Plains Indians. Because they enjoyed a steady source of low-fat, high protein buffalo meat and never stayed in one place for more than one year, they avoided the diseases that were prevalent in the more densely populated cities. We can thus assume that nothing bad would ever befall the Plains Indians.

PRESENT-DAY USA

In the past, stature fell as cities grew, because of overcrowding and increased illness in urban areas. Nowadays, the height gap follows the money. Poorer countries have smaller people.

What's odd is that America hasn't had a growth spurt since World War II. It's possible that there is now such a huge divide between poor and rich in the United States that the average is not affected by a few enormous millionaires —or because fast food is replacing good food during adolescence and reducing the amount of nourishment American children get. So far, the answer is unclear, but either way, it means that there are a lot of us all-American shorties.

THE HOBBITS OF FLORES

Imagine being a *Homo sapien*, wearing a leather jacket and riding your motorcycle around the cul-de-sac in front of your house and suddenly you take a wrong turn and wind up on the island of Flores, midway between Asia and Australia, twelve thousand years ago. On this island, you meet other *H. sapiens* who think you're pretty cool and you become friends with one who speaks present-day English. He tells you of an island nearby where the people are all under three feet tall, the elephants are barely bigger than a horse, the rodents are almost as big as a horse, and the horses are smaller than the komodo dragons that also inhabit the island. Now, slowly open your eyes. Where are you? You're in outer space. No one warned you and it's too late, you don't have a helmet. But wait, you were only dreaming.

The point is, that island that you dreamt about imagining actually exists, and in 2003, a group of Australian and Indonesian anthropologists there stumbled upon evidence of a race of man more hobbit than human. They named the new species *Homo florienses* (man of Flores).

Judging from the fossil remains, *H. florienses* stood just over three feet tall and weighed about fifty-five pounds, which is smaller than any pygmy. (Modern pygmies stand a little under five feet.) They had tiny brains, no chin, and twisted forearms, possibly for climbing and inhabiting trees. Although their brains were smaller than those of *Homo erectus*, who are posited to be their ancestors, they cooked with fire, hunted juvenile stegodons (a kind of pygmy elephant), and built tools.

Even more fascinating is that they survived up until at least 12,000 years ago, when a volcano is thought to have wiped them out.

Some scientists believe that *H. florienses* adaptively shrunk in order to minimize their need for scarce resources on a small island. Others believe that they arrived on the island, possibly on bamboo rafts, already small.

The debate still rages on about whether *H. florienses* was really a different species of human or just a race of *H. sapiens* afflicted with some disease that resulted in their small size, deformed skulls, and tiny brains. Whatever the discovery will end up meaning for science, it provides us with a window into a world that seriously challenges the perspective we accept as normal.

The Incredible Growing and Shrinking Human

Every man at three years old is half his height.
—LEONARDO DA VINCI

HOW FAST YA' GROWIN'?

Humans grow very quickly from birth to age three, at which point growth levels off at a rate of about 1½ inches per year. When humans reach puberty in adolescence, they have another growth spurt (growing at a rate of 2 to 3 inches a year), which is sometimes followed by another bout of gradual growth. When people get older, they start to shrink, which is why older people are grumpy and often wear tall, outdated hats.

HOW FAST YA' SHRINKIN'?

While the majority of our growth differences are based on how much our legs grow, the majority of our shrinking differences are based on how much our backs shrink and hunch. If your back remains straight and tall, but your legs are shrinking, that means you are standing in quicksand.

We start to shrink around the age of forty, when the disks between the vertebrae in our spine start to compress. Another reason some people shrink is because of osteoporosis, which is when spongy bone tissue breaks down and isn't rebuilt. Even if you start to shrink, don't worry—you are so much taller than a baby, it is laughable.

The Longest and Shortest of It

If you're feeling a little too short or a little too tall after reading about average heights throughout the ages, then read on—the following people are *unmistakably* shorter or taller than you. And if that doesn't interest you, read on anyways—the second half of this book is all coupons and personal ads.

THE SHORTEST WOMAN

Lucia Zarate was a 1'8" woman who never weighed more than 5 pounds as an adult. For some perspective, realize that I've eaten steaks that weigh more than 5 pounds. I'm writing this on a computer that is practically 1'8". I've eaten computers that were five steaks thick. I've written my name on a steak and given it to an adoring fan. That should put things in some kind of perspective.

Lucia was born in 1864 in San Carlos, Mexico. She was billed as both "the Greatest Wonder of the Age" and "the Puppet Woman."

THE SHORTEST MAN

Gul Mohammed was the shortest living, mobile man, at 1'10". (There have been shorter men, but they were unable to walk.) Like many dwarfs, his family was of normal height, but Gul weighed *more than all of them combined*. (That last part is not even remotely true. However, it's not so off the mark for another famously small person:

Carrie Akers, 2'11", weighed up to 300 pounds when she was performing with Barnum's Circus.)

THE SHORTEST TWINS?

Maltjus and Bela Matina were Hungarian twins who topped off at 30 inches each. They sold war bonds together in World War I and went by the stage names Mike and Ike Candy. (The candy was named after them.) They performed as Munchkins in *The Wizard of Oz*, and records indicate that they may have had a triplet, Lajos, who went by the name of Leo and played a Munchkin as well. If that's true then they are the world's smallest—and least trustworthy—triplets.

THE SHORTEST COUPLE

Douglas Maistre Breger da Silva, 35", wed Claudia Pereira Rocha, 36", and they became the world's smallest couple. (Barnum's Circus claims some smaller couples, but circus people were notorious for exaggerating—and de-zaggerating.)

THE TALLEST ACTOR

Bart "the Bear" was 9'6" and was in such blockbuster movies as *The Edge* and *Legends of the Fall*. He played the bear in both. (He was a bear.)

[A One Thousand Times Magnification of the Smallest Society Woman Ever Drawn]

The Circus, the Sideshow, and the Beforeshow

The mind, not the body, measures the man.
—CHE-MAH (MEMBER OF P. T. BARNUM'S SHOW)

Step right up! The circus is in town! Just kidding, you're still just reading this book. Although most short people would like to distance themselves from the circus and, more specifically, the "freak show," shorties are an integral part of the circus's past, and our contributions should not be overlooked.

The truth is, I could write a whole book just about the circus. (Note to self: Write a book about trying to write about the circus. Call it *The Elephant's Tears*.)

> Most dwarfs have normal-size heads and torsos but small limbs, whereas proportionate dwarfs are just that—proportionate. Proportionate dwarfs are not born small but they stop growing very early on. The general definition of a dwarf is someone who is 4'10" or under.

THE SIDESHOW, OR P. T. BARNUM'S EXPLOIT-A-TORIUM

A key attraction in sideshows and dime museums were proportionate dwarfs, who at the time were called midgets. (*Midget* is now considered a derogatory term, largely because it dates from this era of "freak shows.")

One of the most famous proportionate dwarfs, the man who catapulted P. T. Barnum to stardom and vice versa, was Charles Sherwood Stratton.

GENERAL TOM THUMB AND HIS WIFE, LAVINIA, INVITE YOU TO READ THIS PARAGRAPH

Charles was likely born on January 4, 1838, although his birth date is often listed as January 1832, because Phineas Barnum first exhibited him as Tom Thumb, an eleven-year-old boy from England, rather than as Charles

> Tom was well known for his impression of Napoleon, which delighted English audiences. Napoleon also enjoyed the impression's merits... from the grave!

Sherwood Stratton, a five-year-old boy from Connecticut. Barnum explained that Americans liked their marvels older and from Europe.

Tom, whose height was somewhere between 25 and 28 inches, performed songs and feats of smallness for Queen Victoria (who gave him a little carriage with four Shetland ponies and a little driver) and many other eminences. He helped make Barnum the most famous sideshow man of all time. Tom married Mary Lavinia Warren Bump, another small wonder in Barnum's show, beating out Commodore Nutt for her affections. Their wedding ceremony was a major event.

AND BABY MAKES THREE?

A picture of the Thumbs with their daughter was published in a widely circulated magazine. The little girl was reported to weigh 3 pounds

at birth, and only 7¾ pounds at the age of one year, when she was taken on an exhibition of Europe. She was said to have died in New York City when two and a half years old. These are incredibly specific facts, considering that the Thumbs had no children. Barnum had borrowed someone else's baby for the picture. That's how you make a circus.

Despite an amazing wedding, Tom Thumb eventually died, severing all hopes of staying married. Lavinia later wed Count Magri, 2'8", another performing proportionate dwarf (who was at one point arrested for having sex with a normal-size woman and refusing to marry her).

OTHER SHORT CIRCUS STARS

Business was booming, as you can tell from the number of other well-known tiny stars of the time:

★ Commodore Nutt   ★ Major Atom
★ Princess Winnie Wee   ★ Admiral Dot**
★ Count Rosebud*   ★ Baron Littlefinger
★ Princess Wee Wee   ★ The Little Esquimaux Lady
★ The Eldorado Dwarf   ★ Commodore Foote

*Later Count Magri
**Often paired with Colonel Goshen, "the Arabian Giant"

Tom Thumb's name came from an old English ballad that began, "In Arthur's court Tom Thumb did live...." The Tom Thumb of the song was literally the size of a thumb, small enough to fit through the holes in Swiss cheese, but there was a very real tradition of proportionate dwarfs attached to the courts of kings.

THE BEFORE SHOW, OR THE ROYAL CIRCUS

During the Roman Empire, proportionate dwarfs were in such high demand as gladiators, entertainers, and servants, it is thought that Romans would actually "manufacture" dwarfs by starving children or constricting their growth somehow (like a Chinese foot-binding, but for the whole body).

Roman emperors and European monarchs would also keep dwarfs as "pets." (It is important to note that

> The Romans had two words for dwarfs: *nanus*, for a naturally born dwarf, and *pumilo* for a dwarf "created" by crazy, dwarf-loving Romans.

some of these rulers were probably dwarfs themselves, although little definite proof exists.) Perhaps the most interesting of these royal favorites was Jeffrey Hudson.

CROSSING THE HUDSON: A BAD IDEA

Jeffrey Hudson (1619–82), was introduced to the Court of Charles I in a pie. Here are just a few of the stories from Hudson's incredibly stormy life:

★ Soon after Queen Henrietta Maria had married Charles I, she was presented with a pie, and out jumped the young eighteen-inch Hudson. (He had not been baked into the pie, as *that* would have been insane.) The queen just *had* to have him, and protected him from then on.

★ In the late 1640s, while in exile in Paris, Hudson challenged a Mr. Crofts to a duel. Crofts arrived with a tiny squirt gun, obviously making fun of Hudson's size, at which point Hudson shot Crofts to death.

★ While on the lam, Hudson was kidnapped by pirates and sold into slavery. He returned to England ten years later, inexplicably twenty-one inches taller.

★ The Flemish portrait painter Sir Anthony Van Dyck painted a portrait of Hudson. It is reported to be so sad that the viewer cannot help but reflect on his or her own shortcomings. That's right—the portrait is a mirror. Actually, there really is a portrait. Pretty cool, huh?

Tallest and Shortest Animals

People aren't the only people on the planet, you know—there are also animals. And height is relative among species as well. When you're feeling low-down, remember that humans are taller than 99 percent of the rest of the world's creatures! (That includes insects and microscopic bacteria, of course.)

Here are some different animal heights for you to stack up against:

CHIMPS: Our closest living relative is the chimpanzee, who measures between 27 and 40 inches. Remember, chimpanzees are our relatives. That means we can't marry them (legally). Please remember that.

THE LARGEST MONKEY: The male mandrill, or man ape, is 24 to 30 inches tall, with a 2- to 3-inch tail. Mandrills have ugly monkey faces, but they are beautiful colors.

THE SMALLEST MONKEY: Fully grown, the pygmy marmoset weighs only 4.2 ounces and measures 5.3 inches. Given those dimensions you might not expect this, but... it can leap over 16 feet into air!

LARGEST PARASITE: The next time someone calls you a parasite because you're short, ask him if he means you're a *Diphyllobothrium latum* or a *Pneumocystis carinii*. If he means the former, then he is actually complimenting you, because that parasite can grow to as long as 30 to 60 feet, living in the small intestines of fish and humans. If he means the latter, then he is calling you the...

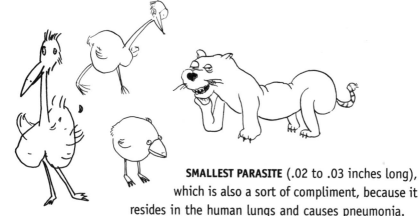

SMALLEST PARASITE (.02 to .03 inches long), which is also a sort of compliment, because it resides in the human lungs and causes pneumonia.

THE LARGEST LAND MAMMAL: The adult male African elephant grows to a height that ranges from 9'10" to 12 feet. That's without shoes on.

BEARS: The smallest bear is the Malayan sun bear, that ranges from 3 feet to 4'6", while a polar bear is 11 feet and a grizzly bear stands at 9 feet. The next time you're grumbling about your view at the movies, thank your lucky stars you're not a sun bear seated behind a grizzly at the bear movie theater. (They also pretty much only show artsy polar bear films—*with subtitles*.)

LARGEST PREHISTORIC RODENT: *Phoberomys pattersoni* (Patterson's mouse of fear, named for its modern-day discoverer) is believed to have weighed 1,500 pounds, and was about the size of a buffalo. It had huge teeth, which were perfect for biting through prehistoric TiVo wires.

SNAKES: Since most other animals don't stand erect, height isn't always the best way to measure them. For instance, a human is much "taller" than the largest snake, the green anaconda, but height doesn't seem to matter when there are 30 to 35 feet of cuddly snake wrapped around you.

SMALLEST ORGANISM TO CAUSE AMNESIA IN HUMANS: The single-celled Pfiesteria piscicida is around .0007 inch. It also...um...what was I saying? Hey—where am I?! I forget my own name!

INSECTS: The giant African millipede is only between 1 and 15 inches long. The emperor scorpion is between 10 and 12 inches long.

Between the giants and the emperors I'm starting to feel better about myself.

SMALLEST CAT EVER: A male blue-point Himalayan Persian named Tinker Toy was 2¾ inches tall and 7½ inches long. He *hated* Mondays.

SMALLEST BIRD: The bee hummingbird of Cuba is 2¼ inches long and has the fastest wing beat of any bird (or human).

LARGEST BIRD: The North African ostrich measures 9 feet tall, stupidly trying to reach the sky by growing rather than flying.

STORK: The Marabou Stork is 5 feet tall—just tall enough to deliver human babies.

UNDERWATER LEVIATHANS

Eighty percent of the world's organisms live under water, including the LARGEST ANIMAL—the blue whale. This guy is about 80 feet long, weighs as much as 40 rhinos, and is 100 million times bigger than the earth's smallest mammal: Kitti's hog-nosed bat.

The LARGEST FISH is the whale shark, at 40 feet long and 11 tons. That's quite a bit bigger than THE SMALLEST SEAHORSE: the pygmy seahorse, .63 inches. It would be hard to ride that "horse." It would also be inadvisable to ride a whale shark.

Giant kelp is the FASTEST GROWING PLANT in the world. In warm water, it can grow two feet a day. Imagine if you grew two feet a day! Imagine if you were a plant!

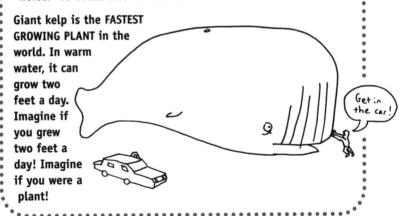

Get in the car!

Tallest and Shortest Aliens

Peegaborg	**7.43 Elmos**
Bumbagoog	**8.9 Glatzgogs**
Nininininizoo	**14.1 Doodiddies**
Nininininitoo	**26,000,000,000 Elmos**
Vicksvaporcub	**44 Inches**

ALIEN HEIGHT F.A.Q.

What is the shortest alien?
Bumbagoog.

What is the tallest alien?
Vicksvaporcub.

Is there heightism among aliens?
Aliens don't discriminate based
on height, they discriminate based
on number of tentacles.

Does height affect number of tentacles?
Number of tentacles is a hereditary trait that is independent of
environment or height.

How do you know this crap?
My brother is an alien, jerk.

The Tallest and Shortest Things in the World

Heck, while we're at it, let's step back and compare our size with some nonliving things in the universe.

THE TALLEST MOUNTAIN: If you measure mountain height from above sea level, then Mount Everest is the tallest, at 29,035 feet. If you measure mountain height from the base to the peak, then Mauna Kea in Hawaii is the tallest, at 33,480 feet; although only 13,796 of them are above sea level. If you measure a mountain's height by the sound of its aura, you are a crazy person.

THE DEEPEST MAN-MADE HOLE: The geological exploratory borehole near Zapolyarny, in arctic Russia, reached a depth of 40,226 feet. Some guy, reading this somewhere and digging a hole to China is pretty discouraged right now.

THE SMALLEST THING: Quarks and leptons are about the smallest things there are. Imagine how small an atom is, and then imagine that it is made out of quarks and leptons. What you are now doing is imagining the truth.

LONGEST ZUCCHINI: A 7'2" zucchini was grown in Hagen, Germany. People who pride themselves on being taller than you should realize that they are still smaller than a zucchini.

THE SHORTEST POEM:

Lines on the Antiquity of Microbes

Adam

Had 'em.

—STRICKLAND GILLIAN

Other contenders are:

Me,
We.

—MUHAMMAD ALI

I
Why?

—CHARLES GHIGNA

LONGEST DAY IN HISTORY: Due to the gravitational effects of the Moon, the Earth's rotation is slowing by about .02 seconds every century, so each day is a tiny, tiny bit longer. That means the longest day in history is today! So if you are twenty years old, you are actually older than your parents were when they were twenty, which means—that's right!—eventually children will be older than their parents!

SHORTEST DAY IN HISTORY: Time flies when you're having fun, so I would say the shortest day was the day that my dad let me come to work with him at the fudge-eating factory.

TALLEST BUILDING: Taipei 101, in Taiwan, is 1,666 feet tall. Luckily, it has elevators. Unluckily, they only go to the second floor. Luckily, the second floor is 1,500 feet above ground. Unluckily, it is full of dragons.

THE SHORTEST CAR: Scientists built a car that is 4 nanometers wide, with buckyballs (spheres of pure carbon, containing sixty atoms each) for wheels. The purpose is to be able to carry molecular material over small spaces and build little nanofactories and such. Great, now all the good jobs in the nanofactories are gonna go to foreign nanoworkers. Thanks, scientists.

THE SHORTEST CAR TRIP: My family was going to go to the Baseball Hall of Fame in Cooperstown, New York, but my brothers and I were fighting so much that my dad turned the car around before we even got to the end of our street. I've heard Cooperstown is really awesome, though.

The Shortest Chapter
in the World

Hello!

PART TWO

Smallotry

Short vs. Tall

Get you gone, you dwarf; you minimus,
of hindr'ing knot-grass made; you bead, you acorn..."
—HELENA IN *A MIDSUMMER NIGHT'S DREAM*,
TO HER FORMER BFF, THE DIMINUTIVE HERMIA

SMALLOTRY

Now that we've put shortness in perspective and we're all feeling a little better about ourselves, let me remind you of why you felt bad about yourself in the first place: you love someone who doesn't love you back. Just kidding—you don't even know what love is. Love is really interesting.

No, the reason you feel bad about yourself, about being short, is because of *smallotry*, or what is commonly known as *heightism*. People knowingly and unknowingly discriminate all the time against those who are short.

Smallotry (I use *smallotry* instead of *heightism* because I made it up) affects us in every facet of our lives: in the places we work, in the media we watch, in the music we listen to, in the people we date, and in the amusement park rides we can't ride. For a more in-depth look at smallotry in our society, read forward. For an in-depth look at the smallest things in the world, read backward.

YOU MUST BE THIS TALL TO READ THIS PAGE

SIX FLAGS (NEW JERSEY)
Superman Ultimate Flight.................54" to 76" in height to ride

PARAMOUNT'S GREAT AMERICA
Top Gun...54" minumum

SANTA CRUZ BEACH BOARDWALK
The Giant Dipper.......................................50" minimum

WALT DISNEY WORLD
Space Mountain.......................................44" minumum

DISNEYLAND PARIS
CyberSpace Mountain...............................51.2" minumum

LEGOLAND
Lego Technic Test Track.............................42" minumum
    (If under 5'2", must be accompanied by a friend 52" or taller)

KNOTT'S BERRY FARM
Montezooma's Revenge.............................48" minumum

UNCLE COSMIC JR'S AMUSEMENT PARK
FOR THE SHORT STATURED

The Limbo.............................Under 64"

Ducking under Turnstiles ....Under 68"

Upside-Down Roller Coaster on the Ground ......Under 50"

The Half–Ferris Wheel ....Under 60"

Low-Ceilinged Merry-Go-Round ....Under 52"

Daffy Dave's Low-Impact,
Slow-Paced Matterhorn ....Under 40"

Krazy Cindy's Chauffered Bumper-Cars
for the Elderly ....Under 58"

Nicknames

Everyone gets teased as a child. You did, I did, even my friend Robby got teased. (Sorry, Rob.) When I was little, there was no end to the "Runt" and "Squish" and "Squid" name-calling. Bullies are known cowards and atheists, but their taunts can really hurt at such an impressionable age.

COMMONLY USED

Runt	Thumbelina
Shorty	Shortstuff
Shrimp	Squirt
Squiggy	Squish
Shortstack	Little Man
Sis	Smallgirl
Kid	Bug
Baby	

Bullies keep short people organized.

RARELY (OR NEVER) USED

Shorty Bonds	Mr. Madagascar
St. Smalls	Bitsy Bill
Shorty McSmall	Professor Baby
Smally McSmall	
Angstrom	
The Amazing Dr. Mini	
Gloria Estesmall	
Spuds Petite	
Florence Piddlywink	
Undersized Alphonse	
Skittle	
Shmeggy	

Bullies use every part of a short person.

BIGotry

Of course, as you know by now, there is no limit to the small-mindedness of some large people. So what do we do about it?

A great man once said, "You can't change the cards you're dealt but you can choose how to play the hand." Another great man once said, "A full house beats two pair, so gimme all yer money, you son-of-a-gun."

A bully in action.

The point is, as with all adversities, there are a number of positive ways to cope, but those are all boring, so here are some good nicknames you can use for tall people, courtesy of me.

El Grande	Stiltbelly	Too Tall
Tallbones	Smoked Ham	Gigabyte
Skyscraper	Slim Jim	Elephantasy
Birds-Eye-Vaughan	Dr. Brontosaurus	Swamp Thing
André the Giant	Ladderlegs	Humongstress
Pete the Giant (André's brother)	Gigantro	Charlotte Bronco

A SAMPLE FIGHT BETWEEN A TALL AND SHORT PERSON

TALL PERSON: Hey, Shorty Bonds, get me some milk. Oh yeah, you can't reach. My bad.

SHORT PERSON: Luckily you can reach anything, Ladderlegs, except the ground.

TALL PERSON: Oh man, sorry. You're not short. You're vertically challenged.

SHORT PERSON: Guess what, Humongstress, you're socially challenged.

TALL PERSON: Why would you say something so hurtful, Professor Baby?

SHORT PERSON: Now you know how it feels, Dr. Brontosaurus.

BONUS TALL PERSON'S NICKNAME PAGE, COURTESY OF SHAQUILLE O'NEAL

Shaq, 7'1", is an enormous basketball player and he gives himself a lot of nicknames. Most of these can be used to refer to any tall person, but some are pretty Shaq-specific.

The Diesel   The Big Aristotle   The Big Daddy
The Big Baryshnikov   Doctor Shaq*

*Shaq gave himself this name after earning his MBA, which, of course, does not make him a doctor.

Earl Boykins scolds a naughty Shaq.

Natural Selection

et's face it: being tall is pretty desirable. Tall people take up more space. They seem massive and impressive. During the Renaissance, people built tall towers to be closer to God—they didn't build holy ranch houses. Tall people make love in a different and fascinating way that puts the way short people make love to shame. To be tall is to be bathed in the warm glow of heaven from birth to death—which only rarely comes to the very tall.

Or so it seems. It is not entirely a matter of arbitrary aesthetics (or divine provenance) though; there is some basis for height desirability in natural selection theory.

PRIMITIVE INSTINCTS

Natural selection proposes that beings pick mates with traits that are best suited to provide their offspring with the means for survival. To see how this relates to humans, let's look at a testimonial from a beautiful *Homo habilis* woman:

> *I had just reached marrying age and I had two suitors, Crampook and Vistacazoo. Now, I need a man who is strong and will be able to hunt saber-toothed tigers for me and protect me from other saber-toothed tigers. He needs to be able to lift large boulders, to make a cave dwelling for me and our children, and he needs to be able to wrestle any orangutans who owe him money. Crampook is small, like a nerd, whereas Vistacazoo is tall and powerfully built. He is the man who will ensure my survival in these harsh elements and he will provide for and protect us. Vistacazoo is my man. We are "in love."—Linda*

So you see, tallness is very desirable in a harsh physical world. Because being tall is helpful to survival, the trait has been passed down. However, small men and women find mates as well. There are many traits that make a person desirable. But you don't need to hear it from me. Just read this testimonial from a different, buxom *H. habilis* woman:

I am very physically attractive. I know this because of how the town toughs, Thog and Krukshank, talk about me. Many men show me their eyes and give to me gifts of pelts and bracelets of human hair. It is my wide birthing hips and ample breasts that tell them that I will provide large and

A beautiful ballet of line & texture.

Not as good.

healthy children who will not want for milk. However, not all of the men show me equal attention. There is, of course, Balkazar, who is very tall. I know deep down that he has reached his height because he has been well nourished and never suffered sickness—surely I would want to give my children a father with a healthy set of genes, so they have the potential to be just as healthy and to have children of their own. Then, I shan't forget, there is Ugalug, who is not nearly so tall but has a very symmetrical face. I also know that a symmetrical face is a sign of good health, and so that is also attractive to me. Although Ugalug cannot hunt nearly so well as Balkazar, he is quick witted with men, and can convince them to give him food so long as he does their taxes. In this way, he will provide for my children. Also, and most important, he listens to me and has a good sense of humor. He once made me laugh so hard that a saber-toothed tiger tooth came out of my nose and almost killed both of us. This made him laugh very hard—and then he kissed me. Ugalug has very sensuous lips, and I realize that this is a quality I also find very attractive.—Emily

LOVING LARGE IN THE PRESENT

Fast-forward thousands of years, and things haven't changed that much. Nowadays, when a woman looks at a tall man and subconsciously sees a good provider, she is still not so far off. While he may not hunt down and kill a mammoth for her (although he might; I don't know very much about tall people and they generally frighten me), he might very well bring home a mammoth in the modern sense (bringing home the bacon).

The Business of Being Tall

From as far back as the early 1900s, many studies have shown that taller men and women have better jobs, earn more money, and move up the ladder quicker than short people do. When given identical résumés on which the only difference was height, the vast majority of employers said they would choose to hire the taller candidate. When given identical résumés on which the only difference was flavor, most employers chose the strawberry résumés. (Only two employers chose the nutmeg, and one very healthy employer chose broccoli. As you can see, this was a very important study.)

There is little evidence to suggest that taller people are more competent, creative, or commanding at their jobs (just ask 5'7" crazy billionaire Ross Perot!), so is this merely an example of economic smallotry? Possibly. One theory is that employers subconsciously discriminate against short people while seeing taller people as natural leaders.

SHORT PEOPLE DON'T LIKE THEMSELVES ENOUGH

Height gives people social confidence, or at least makes them seem more confident to others. There is something inherently more dignified about being able to speak over

SHORT TEEN BLUES

Recent studies suggest that it is not one's adult height, but rather one's height as an adolescent that determines job success. Taller teens are cooler so they make friends, play sports, and learn how to socialize. Short teens are losers who collect stingrays and write books about being short. Thus, even if a short adolescent eventually outgrows his or her tall teenage peers, he or she might never reap the economic benefits of being tall.

the sneeze-guard at the sandwich counter than having to stand on a stool and scream your order. It goes deeper than that, though.

SHORT PEOPLE ARE UGLY

Tallness is considered physically attractive, and studies also show that attractive people, regardless of height, also earn more, get hired more easily, and promoted more often than unattractive people.

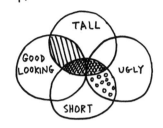

Appearance- Success Chart

Key:

\\\\   What you want to be

∷   You don't want to be this

✿   These are impossible

SHORT PEOPLE ARE STUPID

While you will soon see that many of the world's greatest geniuses, artists, and thinkers were short, a recent study by Anne Case and Christina Paxson* concludes that, on average, taller people get better jobs and salaries because they are more intelligent than short people. Yes, you read that correctly! Now, I know this is supposed to be an "empowering" book but, come on, people, I'm not your mother. Data shows that taller people score better on cognitive tests at every age. Why? I wish I knew, but the bulk of the argument is explained in symbols and equations that I have no hope of understanding because I am only 5'3".

Here are some less well-researched possibilities:

SHORT PEOPLE ARE NOTORIOUS DRUNKS

Self-explanatory.

---

*Does this really seem like the kind of book that has footnotes? I can't believe you even looked down here. Well, now I sort of feel guilty, like I should at least make this worth your while. Um...what would be good...I know. Here are four digits from my credit card number, in no particular order: 4, 2, 5, 8.

SHORT PEOPLE LOVE FLOWERS

It's hard for anyone to get any work done when there are flowers all over the place and a bunch of colleagues talking about how nice all the beautiful flowers are.

SHORT PEOPLE ARE GRUFF

Not all short people, but I know of at least three who are way too gruff.

EXPENSIVE INCHES

It is pretty commonly accepted that an increase of one inch in height is equivalent to an increase of between 400 and 800 dollars a year. (Others say each inch = a 2 to 2.5 percent increase in salary.) That means that a 6' man or woman will earn at least $100,000 more than will his or her 5'6" colleague in his or her lifetime.

5'2" 5'7" 6'8"

Job Interviews

So tall people get all the good gigs? Let's look at two examples of a typical job interview with a short person, and two with a tall person. See if you can figure out which interview is which.

Scene 1

INTERVIEWER: I don't know, they're *your* parents, *you* kill them. That's great, oh, listen, I have to call you back, someone is here for an interview. [hangs up phone]

APPLICANT [enters]:

INTERVIEWER: ...

APPLICANT: ...

INTERVIEWER: ...

APPLICANT: ...Um, hello?

INTERVIEWER: Please have a seat.

APPLICANT: Thanks.

INTERVIEWER: ...

APPLICANT: ...

INTERVIEWER: ...

APPLICANT: ...

INTERVIEWER: ...

APPLICANT: So, I'm very excited—

INTERVIEWER: Get the hell out of my office.

Scene 2

APPLICANT:
Good morn—

INTERVIEWER:
You're hired.

Scene 3

INTERVIEWER: Hello Mr. Short...er...Mr. Johnson.

APPLICANT: Um, it's Mrs. Ross.

INTERVIEWER: What's that? Oh. Right. *Of course.* Now, am I correct in assuming that you have never held a job before?

APPLICANT: No. You would be incorrect.

INTERVIEWER: Let's do a little role-playing here, you with me so far?

APPLICANT: I'm with you. Yes.

INTERVIEWER: Great. Okay, I'm in the bathroom flossing. Suddenly I start to choke.

APPLICANT: On the floss?

INTERVIEWER: It's unclear. I use a lot of floss.

APPLICANT: You just stuff the floss down your throat?

INTERVIEWER: Some of it. The rest I save. That's beside the point. I'm choking on the floor of the men's room and no one is around. I try to scream, but no one can hear me.

APPLICANT: And I come in and save you?

INTERVIEWER: No, you can't hear me. In fact, you're out sick.

APPLICANT: Then what role am I playing?

INTERVIEWER: You play the angel of death, who delivers divine justice for the crimes I have committed against the lord.

APPLICANT: Um—

INTERVIEWER: Deliver me swiftly!

APPLICANT: Hyah!

INTERVIEWER: ...

APPLICANT: ...

INTERVIEWER: Was that a karate chop?

APPLICANT: Uh, I guess it was.

INTERVIEWER: The angel of death administers the fatal blow with a karate chop?

APPLICANT: Sure. Maybe not.

INTERVIEWER: Wow, I should think not. [writes something on a pad of paper]

APPLICANT [straightens out blazer]: So...

INTERVIEWER: Yes, I'm afraid you're just simply too short.

Scene 4

INTERVIEWER: Please have a seat.

APPLICANT: I'm already sitting.

INTERVIEWER: You're already...by God, you *are* already sitting, my goodness. Oh my goodness. This is truly outstanding!

APPLICANT: Beg pardon?

INTERVIEWER: No need, no need my dear woman! Now, let me look at your, ahem, qualifications...

APPLICANT: I'm six foot four.

INTERVIEWER: What leadership!

APPLICANT: I'm six foot six in heels.

INTERVIEWER: What drive!

APPLICANT: I'm eight foot ten on stilts.

INTERVIEWER: Hmm. Decent. Well, I have to ask you a few more questions. Just a formality, really.

APPLICANT: I beg you do not.

INTERVIEWER: These shouldn't be too hard. What would you say are your strengths?

APPLICANT: I am terrible at driving.

INTERVIEWER: ...Interesting. And, what would you say is your greatest weakness?

APPLICANT: I am lazy. I drink too much water. I eat too much sometimes and other times not enough. I cannot regulate my own body temperature, like a reptile. I require constant praise and an equal dose of constant degradation. Insects are attracted to me, sexually. I lived in a tree for five years because I could not find the ground and I lived underground for another five years because I was so depressed about leaving the tree. When I have an idea it causes actual lightbulbs to shatter. The same thing happens when I don't have an idea but am just breathing too heavily. Rainbows hate me. I have a tendency to fall in love with men that have been dead for centuries. Every Tuesday I rent a double-decker tour bus and give myself imaginary tours of the stars' homes, which may or may not involve me smoking crack in the driver seat of a double-decker bus. I age backward, like Merlin. Books confuse me but magazines make me angry for not being more like books. I don't believe in the death penalty. Like, I don't believe that it exists. Both of my eyes are fake, but if I find true love they will become real again. Have you heard of the *Titanic*? I have never even heard of it. Every year I send God a postcard of myself naked and I have never once gotten a response. I am technically in a coma. I need the lottery explained to me every single night. I think the weather is debatable.

INTERVIEWER: ...so...six foot six in heels?

APPLICANT: Nine foot six when I stand on top of a car.

INTERVIEWER: When can you start?

Booby Trapping Your Office

HOW TO BOOBY TRAP THE OFFICE TO GET BACK AT TALL PEOPLE

★ Rig trip wires all over the place.
★ Hang up a sign that says "Free sensual massage" with an arrow; there is a pit full of alligators underneath.
★ Superglue a tall person's hand to his stapler.
★ Superglue a tall person's most valuable possessions to his desk and set fire to the office.
★ Have some kind of a freak-out and blame the government (I tried this one, it worked maybe half).
★ You can never have enough trip wires.
★ Flush all the toilets at the same time. That will really embarrass the tall guy who never flushes.
★ Experiment with crossbreeding and produce horrible mutations of animals. Then name them after the tallest people in your office.

★ Demand some goddamn respect.
★ Demand some goddamn piggyback rides.

How an Office Is ...

for Short People

Quiz: The Vast Tall-Wing Media Conspiracy

S ure, short people and tall people hate each other equally, but for some reason being short is accepted as worse. Is this because, as Case and Paxson suggest (see fake footnote on page 55), short people are dumber than tall people? Sure, if intelligence is measured by hat size. Sorry. That is disrespectful to the tall person who is ghost-writing this book for me while I eat Play-Doh and try to get Scotch tape out of my hair.

The answer is, it's the media's fault. Whether it's stereotyping short people as comic-relief buffoons, wimpy sidekicks, hilariously small evil madmen, or feisty Napoleons who pathetically strive for dignity, the media has not done much to help short people's self-esteem. Here's a quiz designed to test...something or other. No need to cheat—I included the answer after each question.

Media Quiz

1. WHICH IS FUNNIER?

A. A tall person telling a short person what to do.
B. A short person telling a tall person what to do.
C. Two short people living happily together.
D. A tall person's pants falling down, causing him to fall in a well.
E. A short person falling down a well, catching pneumonia, and upon recovery spending the rest of her life donating time and resources to philanthropic causes.

ANSWER: This was a trick question. B is the funniest because it is incongruous for a tall person to be at the mercy of a short person.

The rest of the options cancel each other out for a variety of reasons that I couldn't ask you to understand.

2. WHICH THREE OF THESE MOVIE PARTS WOULD A SHORT PERSON MOST LIKELY HAVE?

A. Knight
B. King
C. Evil king
D. Princess
E. Queen
F. Queen's mother
G. A baby
H. Court jester
I. A flower

ANSWER: C, F, and H are all acceptable. Short people are usually elderly, evil, or comedic characters, not leading men or ladies (even though many leading roles are played by short actors and actresses). I put in I. because my grandson played a flower in his school play. What, you didn't realize I had a grandson? He's fifteen, and single, ladies.

3. WHICH ONE IS THE SHORTEST?

a.   b.   c.   d.

ANSWER: They are all approximately the same size.

4. WHICH OF THESE TV SITCOM CHARACTERS IS THE BUTT OF ENDLESS SHORT JOKES?

A. Carlton from *The Fresh Prince of Bel Air*
B. Radar from *M.A.S.H.*
C. Charlie Rose

ANSWER: Both Carlton and Radar are ridiculed for being short. Each, at one point, tried to garner respect by wearing elevator shoes only to find out that they didn't work, but teaching everyone else a valuable lesson in the process. Charlie Rose is just immensely respected in his profession. Not short.

5. WHICH OF THESE QUALITIES ARE MOST OFTEN USED IN CONJUNCTION WITH SHORTNESS TO PORTRAY AN UNATTRACTIVE CHARACTER?

A. Fatness
B. Baldness
C. Angriness
D. Glasses
E. Smelliness
F. Pugilisticness
G. Languorousness
H. Tallness

ANSWER: A, B, C, D, E, F, G, and H.

6. IT IS ACCEPTABLE FOR A POLITICIAN, BUSINESSMAN, OR CELEBRITY TO MAKE FUN OF SOMEONE FOR HIS OR HER:

A. Race
B. Class
C. Sick mother
D. Gender
E. Disability
F. Shortness

ANSWER: Just F. Maybe in some scenarios C, if the politician is making fun of his brother, and they are alone, and they know that their mom is going to be okay.

> SHORT FRIENDS: **Any TV or movie character with a variation on the name Buddy or Bud is guaranteed to be short, except for Giantbud Buddington Giant III, from the daytime soap *Giants of Our Big Lives*.**

7. WOULD YOU RATHER BE:

A. A comic relief character
B. Leading lady
C. Helpful alien
D. Leading man
E. Rapping, break-dancing grandma

ANSWER: As a short person on a crusade to earn short people the respect they deserve, I hope that you chose either A, B, C, or D, depending on your personality. If you chose E, so help me God...

YOUR SCORE: You should have gotten 100 percent, unless you were deliberately going back after finding out the correct answers and changing your answers to be wrong. I used to do this a lot on other people's tests when I was a teacher in a high school. That is one reason teaching high school shouldn't be considered "community service," especially if you have to do community service for exposing yourself to a bunch of high school students.* I've ruined a lot of lives.

SHORTLIGHT ON... DANNY DEVITO

DeVito, 5'0", wins a prize for consistently playing the short, unattractive guy. In the old sitcom *Taxi*, he played the lecherous, hot-tempered, evil boss Louie. In the movie *Batman Returns*, he played the hideous, half-human villain called "the Penguin." In the movie *Twins*, he literally played human refuse.

Famous Monster, Danny DeVito

A Brief Plot Synopsis of the Movie *Twins*

Medical experimenters try to create a superhuman, a perfect man, using two embryos. One resulting infant gets all the good DNA and the other gets all the bad DNA. Julius Benedict, played by Arnold Schwarzenegger, is the lucky twin. He is tall, handsome, kind, and smart. Vincent Benedict, played by Danny DeVito, is not so lucky: he is short, fat, bald, stupid, and mean. He is made out of all of the left-over bad things a person can be. Thus, to the makers and supporters of this movie, being short makes you akin to human refuse. Danny DeVito, how could you?

---

*I feel bad about this digression. Here are 4 more numbers from my credit card: 6, 3, 2, 4.

A Standard Formula for a Movie About a Short Person

A short kid is at school.

A bully makes fun of him and stuffs him in his locker.

The kid finagles his way out and makes it to class.

The teacher says, "Marvin, now you're short *and* late. Detention."

In the lunchroom, Marvin is sitting with his only friend, a tall, nerdy, fat kid. A bully comes over and asks Marvin what girl he likes. Marvin is bad at taking social cues and tells the bully honestly which girl he likes. Marvin watches as the bully walks over to the girl and talks to her, pointing at Marvin. All the girls around her start giggling and she looks at Marvin and she throws up.

The bell rings and Marvin gets up to go to class but, before he can, the girl he likes is wheeled over to him in a wheelchair. She is hooked up to an IV. "Marvin, you did this to me," she says. "You ruined my life by embarrassing me because you are so short. This is what happens when you, Marvin, love someone."

She is wheeled off to a waiting ambulance.

Marvin's tall nerdy fat friend asks if Marvin is going to finish his fries.

In gym class two boys are picking teams for baseball. They pick everyone except Marvin, even a kid who is sick.

"Okay, you have to pick an umpire," says the teacher, "and the umpire equipment is so small that it will only fit on Marvin."

"I will be the umpire," says Rick.

"Then who will be your pitcher?"

"We'll play without a pitcher," says Rick. "Now someone help me squeeze into this equipment."

After the first inning Rick takes off his mask, walks over to the bleachers, and calls Marvin "out for life."

In the hallway a pretty girl Marvin has never seen before asks him to the big dance. Marvin says "yes" before realizing she is talking to someone over his head. He turns around and sees that she is talking to his own dad.

"Life is hard, son," says his dad.

Marvin joins the varsity football team to show everyone he is not too small.

Everyone cheers for him.

Within minutes, one of his legs is broken and then the other, followed shortly by the rest of the bones in his body.

Marvin wakes up. He is in a wheelchair at the prom, in a tuxedo. The song "Last Dance" is playing.

Marvin sees the girl he likes, still wheelchair bound because of *her* fall.

He asks her to dance. She smiles through her brand-new dental braces.

They hold hands as the music changes to "Somewhere" from *West Side Story*.

Credits.

After the credits, Marvin holds up two fingers to show that there will be a sequel.

Now, Finally, We'll Talk About Randy Newman

We can be honest here as we're among friends—we all love Randy Newman. He has composed the soundtrack for every Tom Hanks and/or Penny Marshall movie you've ever seen, not to mention every Disney movie (or really any movie about friends). He's like the Andrew Lloyd Webber of raspy songs about friendship, or like the Mozart of crap.

That said, we short people have a few grievances we'd like to air. In 1977, Randy Newman composed a song called "Short People," which includes lyrics implying that short people have no reason to live. (And dirty minds, too.)

It would seem as though Mr. Newman has a real gripe with us. Alas, as in all great art there is a difference between appearance and reality. Randy was actually being *ironic*.

> **A DEFINITION OF IRONY**
> The use of words to convey a meaning that is the opposite of their literal meaning.

Believe it or not, a lot of people dislike other people because of the way they think or look, and Randy thought that a song was a good way to show the fallacy in this sort of thinking. He astutely realized that if he wrote a song about hating African-American or Jewish or Chinese people, he would be in a lot of trouble. As a solution, he chose to ironically make fun of short people since that just didn't seem so bad.

THE SHORT COMMUNITY DISAGREED

Short people were enraged. They protested Newman so much that his song became a huge hit. Now here's the thing, short people: lighten up. The song, even if it is annoying musically, is just a song and it is supposed to be ironic.

BUT HERE'S THE OTHER THING

Some people do dislike and mistreat other people because they are short. And it was not only short people who didn't realize the song was ironic—tall people took the song seriously, too, and it only fueled their intolerance of short people.

AND LIKE I SAID BEFORE

The song is pretty annoying.

Short "Jokes"

Why are people so cruel? One reason is that a lot of taller people think they are being funny, and don't realize they are being hurtful. Even adults think it is acceptable and cute to say things like "stand up" to a short person *who is already standing up*, or they think it is a joke when they call someone "shrimp." Anyway, people make a lot of jokes about short people. In the name of literary criticism, here are some popular short jokes from the Internet, accompanied by my analyses:

You're so short, you gotta stand up to sit down. **That's pretty good. Sort of hard to figure out how it works, but it's pretty catchy.**

You're so short, I'm nuts over you. **Pretty gross pun, but effective.**

You're so short, you bump your head when you try to jump over the subway turnstile. **I like it. Why wouldn't a short person just go under the turnstile? Makes you think. It's mysterious.**

You're so short that you are just 0.00000000000000000000000001% of Yao Ming. **Enigmatic. Clearly someone that small could not exist, so perhaps the shortness is tangential, and the percentage given refers to another, more ephemeral quality of Mr. Ming's.**

You're so short you can walk on stilts and wear a high hat and still walk under a pregnant ant. **I think this is my favorite joke. Everything is covered. I assume a high hat is a kind of top hat. I don't know. I don't care. The perfect joke.**

You're so short that if you walked across the edge of a razor blade you'd look like an ant crossing an eight-lane highway. **Another ant joke. Less successful. Still, a staggering conception of scale.**

You're so short you could walk between the pages of a closed book. **That is very short indeed.**

You're so short, the doctor measured you and put down your height as a negative number. **Solid joke. Stupid doctor, but solid joke.**

You're so short, you could hang glide on a Dorito chip. **I have never seen a Dorito chip float or glide, so I find it hard to believe that additional weight would suddenly improve its aerodynamic properties.**

You're so short, you could be a teller at a piggy bank. **No short person can argue with this.**

You are so short, you play handball on the curb. **Pretty short.**

You're so short, you play racquetball on the curb. **Well, sure, that's where I** *would* **play if I had any time, what with all my handball engagements.**

You are so short, you surf on a Popsicle stick. **No matter what the scale, a Popsicle stick is not proportional to a surfboard. Nonetheless, I can think of some situations where it would be handy.**

You are so short, your homies are the Keebler Elves. **I thought this joke was the work of one person, but it actually appears in several different places. I'm pretty sure this is the work of the Keebler corporation, because who else would be trying to promote the idea that the Keebler Elves were "homies"?**

You are so short, you do backflips under the table. **Incredible talent!**

You are so short, you can swim in a puddle. **Granted.**

You are so short, you might drown in a deep puddle. **Um... sure, if I was unconscious. We've already established that I can swim in a puddle of any depth. But sure, I might. Anyone might. It's a crazy world out there.**

Fairies and Gnomes and Trolls, Oh My!

Television and movies teach us that short people are funny, mean, ugly, greedy, lecherous, and old. That's to be expected: the people who make television and movies have no souls. But even before we're old enough to watch TV without running into the screen trying to hug Bryant Gumbel, our elders read us fairy tales and tell us myths from oral tradition. In these, short people are depicted as monsters.

DWARVES are a mythological race (not to be confused with people with the medical condition dwarfism) of short, bearded miners who live underground in the mountains of Scandinavia and Germany. In Norse mythology, the gods created dwarves from maggots found in the carcass of Ymir, the father of all the giants.

Disclaimer: Some of the following may not be entirely accurate to everyone's exact tradition. Why? Because at some point people made all this stuff up.

The actual origin of dwarves in human minds is a different matter. One theory is that during the Bronze Age, miners from Southern Europe came to the north to look for resources. Their dark skin, short stature, and knowledge of metallurgy and advanced weaponry might have made them seem monstrous and magical to the less-developed people in the north.

THE MINE DWARVES OF CORNWALL warn humans of danger by knocking on mine walls. If not given food, however, they will actually cause walls to cave in. Likewise, **GERMANIC KOBOLDS** and their English counterpart, **BROWNIES**, do housework at night but, if not fed, cause minor accidents to befall the household.

These fairy-tale creatures, who are short enough to live among humans undetected, are often used to explain clumsiness or the failure of machinery. Even in the early twentieth century, fighter pilots used to blame plane malfunctions on tiny gremlins. It would be much harder to accept that a seven-foot ogre had come into your house and knocked over your dishes, or that a magical blue whale climbed into the engine of your plane and removed a few bolts.

> **What Was Tolkien Tokin'?** **What do you have when you have more than one dwarf or elf? A problem! No, you have dwarfs or elfs. It was J. R. R. Tolkien (5'5"), the author of *The Hobbit* and *The Lord of the Rings* trilogy, who first spelled these mythical plurals as dwarves and elves, and that is how many people spell them today. You know, the many people who are always writing about dwarves and elves hanging out everywhere.**

LEPRECHAUNS are tiny mischievous creatures from Ireland who are primarily cobblers. They will lead you to a pot of gold if you catch them, but if you take your eye off them for even an instant, they will vanish. That is why they trick you into looking away. That, and your breath stinks.

ELVES are tiny, attractive humanoids, more attractive than any human. They love to dance in the moonlight and lure humans to dance with them. The humans either disappear or are found dead by morning—so don't dance with elves! I can't stress this enough!

GNOMES are like trolls and dwarves but they wear conical hats and have long white beards. Some people think the sunlight turns them to stone, but oddly there is little proof of this. This belief is bolstered by the prevalence of those garden gnome statues, which were crafted in the mid-1800s in Thuringia, Germany. A really good place for a garden gnome would be Versailles, or Florida.

> Here's a fun game: Try to convince yourselves that elves and goblins and leprechauns exist. Did you? If so, then you might just be imaginative.

LESZY (or Leshy, or Lesij) are found in Slavic forests and can change their size from that of a blade of grass to a towering tree. The Leszy is king of the forest, and often wears its shoes backward. Passersby are encouraged to turn their clothes and shoes around as well, as a sign of respect. (I also do this whenever I see a police officer, so that my babies will be born right-handed.)

EEYEEKALDUK is a small, dark, creature known by the Inuit people as the god of medicine and good health. In other words, they believe that a swarthy Woody Allen represents the epitome of robustness.

KURUPIRA was feared by Brazilian natives as the miniature protector of wild game. Jimmy Buffett was feared by the natives as the laid-back protector of Margaritas.

SHREK was not short at all. Shrek was a big ogre in a big fancy animated movie (adapted from a beautiful book by William Steig) who marries a princess because she doesn't care about what he looks like on the outside, she only cares about what he is like on the inside. Love transcends the physical.

Or does it? The bad guy in this movie, as in so many movies, is extremely short. Lord Farquaad is evil, ambitious, and quick to anger, and is supposedly hilarious that the princess would have to marry him since he is so short. It is fine for her to marry a literal monster, but to marry a short man is considered the height of comedy.

Napoleon and His Amazing Complex

NAPOLEON COMPLEX F.A.Q.

Q. What is the Napoleon complex?

A. It is the common term for a kind of inferiority complex that comes from being of diminutive stature.

Q. Please elaborate.

A. The psychologist Alfred Adler used the emperor, Napoleon Bonaparte, as an example of a person with an inferiority complex based on his short stature, who compensated for this self-perceived weakness by parading around as if he owned the world—and then taking over half of it.

Q. What are some symptoms of the Napoleon complex?

A. Feistiness, aggressiveness, hot-temperedness, megalomania, cockiness, boasting, ambition, refusal to fail, drive to succeed, needing to prove yourself.

Q. How do I know if I...if I have it?

A. It is often accompanied by a fever, or the mumps.

Q. How short do I have to be to have a Napoleon complex?

A. It depends. In professional sports, athletes are often said to have it even if they are 5'9" or 5'10". Napoleon himself was not actually all that short, by the way.

Q. Wait, hold up. I think you made a mistake. You said Napoleon wasn't short?

A. That's right...

NAPOLEON'S HEIGHT

Napoleon is and will forever be known and ridiculed for his short stature. He stood 5'2"—short, to be sure—but keep in mind that he was 5'2" in French inches, which were slightly larger than the British inches we are familiar with today. Napoleon's actual height was more around 5'6½", while the average Frenchman of his day was around 5'4" or 5'5".

The British hated Napoleon, and when they heard that he was 5'2", they ran with it, knowing full well it was a mistranslation of units. In addition, people misinterpreted the idiomatic French term of endearment "Le Petit Caporal" to literally mean "the small general," rather than "the dear general." Also, Napoleon surrounded himself with large guards, who would have made him seem smaller.

His autopsy confirms his average height. Before the autopsy, Napoleon's physician, Francesco Antommarchi, measured the emperor's body as 1.686 meters, which is around 5'6.3" in today's inches.

But the myth took hold. Here is one inaccurate account of Napoleon's state at the time of his death from a 1930s magazine:

> *His pituitary gland was sub-normal. This gave him his short stature and effeminate body. His buttocks were rounded very much*

Napoleon

like a woman's; his skin was white and delicate; the body and pubic hair were scarce, and the hair on his head was thin, fine, and silky. His sex organs were very small. The post-mortem report of Dr. Henry said that the size of the genitals "seemed to exhibit a physical cause for the absence of sexual desire and the chastity which had been stated to have characterized the deceased..."

This just goes to show that it's been hard for Napoleon to catch a break ever since he keeled over, vomiting black blood. Although most of this account is suspect, Dr. Henry was actually at the autopsy, and he did report on the general's small genitals and effeminate, hairless body. Those small genitals are rumored to have been stolen during the autopsy as well. After losing his tiny junk, Napoleon was buried, only to be exhumed twenty years later, due to suspicions of poisoning. While sensationalists and scientists alike persist to this day that he was poisoned, it is likely that he merely died of complications with his treatment for stomach cancer.

ALL RIGHT ALREADY, WHAT'S THE COMPLEX?

Okay, so judging from our biography of Napoleon, it seems like we're ready for a new definition of the Napoleon complex.

> **THE NAPOLEON COMPLEX: A condition whereby a person, through ambition, cunning, ruthlessness, great military and political skill, small genitals, the creation of a codified set of laws, the discovery of the Rosetta Stone, and fine, silky hair, overcompensates for having missed dinner as a child by taking over half of the world and pretending to sleep with a bunch of women.**

Short Conqueror Honorable Mentions

RUNNER-UP: ALEXANDER THE GREAT

LIVED: Fourth century BC

HEIGHT: Probably 5′6″–5′7″ Some believe that he was 5′2″ because of some armor found in a Macedonian tomb that is thought to be his. However, this is unlikely, because Alexander would not have been able to fight effectively on foot (which he often did) if he had been at such a great height disadvantage.

Shortest and Tallest Estimated Heights

Napoleon: 5′2″ — 5′7″

Alexander the Great: 5′2″ — 5′8″

Attila the Hun: 4′6″ — 10′2″

TEACHER: Aristotle

FATHER: King Phillip II of Macedon

HOW HIS FATHER DIED: Alexander's mom probably had Dad killed so Alexander could become king. No evidence of this, but I have some good leads.

DID HE CUT THE GORDIAN KNOT IN TWAIN, INSTEAD OF UNRAVELING IT, TO BECOME THE PROPHESIED CONQUEROR OF ASIA? Yes, according to legend.

WHAT OTHER STUFF DID HE CONQUER: Persia. Egypt. India. Whatever.

FAVORITE PIZZA TOPPING: Hawaiian

QUOTES: "My son, seek thee out a kingdom equal to thyself; Macedonia has not room for thee."—Phillip to Alexander after Alexander tamed the wild stallion Bucephalus.

SEXUAL ORIENTATION: Whoever was around. Guys, girls, the Gordian Knot. Just a chill dude.

ANCESTORS: Achilles, Hercules

DESCENDANTS: Three of the four original Monkees (not Peter Tork).

OVERALL: 8

SECOND RUNNER-UP: ATTILA THE HUN

NICKNAME: The Scourge of God

LIVED: Fifth century AD

HEIGHT: 4'6". Some say he was a dwarf (4'6" is technically a dwarf) but as with all controversial characters, everyone who hated him— Europeans and Romans—would have tried to paint him as an absurd figure, i.e., short.

UNCLE: King Roas. Attila, along with his brother Bleda, inherited their scattered kingdom of Scythian hordes from Roas, who had won them playing bingo.

CONQUERED: Attila was more into plundering and wiping out nations in his path, and some of those include Austria, Germany, and many parts of the Eastern Roman Empire. Pope Leo I himself had to persuade Attila not to sack Rome.

HOW HE DIED: Choked on his own blood on his wedding night. Attila was not a serious drinker, so after getting all lit up at the reception, he ended up passed out on the floor of his conjugal tent. While passed out flat on his back, either his nose started bleeding or his esophagus started hemorrhaging, and he choked on the blood. So when people complain about married life, they are *not* kidding.

OVERALL: 7

WHO WOULD WIN: NAPOLEON, ALEXANDER THE GREAT, OR ATTILA THE HUN?

Attila the Hun would win in a physical fight but Alexander the Great would win in a spelling bee. Napoleon had too weak a stomach for either of those activities.

PART THREE

Profiles in Shortage

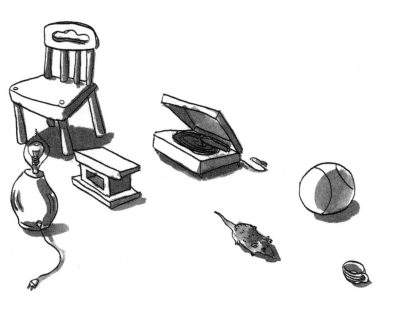

No Small Measure

Fans have never recognized me before because
I'm in newspaper and on radio, two things
where I'm completely anonymous. —WILL SHORTZ

Here's the deal: we can commiserate all day long about being short—how we're treated in the workplace, the media, on the dating scene, in fairy tales, you name it. We can rent a cabin in Vermont, or I even know a nice place in Maine by a lake where we can build a campfire, you and I, drink some whiskey, howl at the moon, write our names in the snow, and really work through our issues. Why aren't we paid more? Why is man so cruel to his fellow, shorter man? Are you Danny DeVito? Are you *actual human refuse*?

On the other hand, we could just look at how many celebrated short people there are in the world, and marvel. This is a list of people, like you and me, who tread water in the shallow end of the pool, even while they are painting and acting and singing and dancing with the rest of their little bodies. That is maybe not the best metaphor. Put another way, you are going to be shocked by which famous people are short. And after the shock wears off, a flood of joy will wash over you as you realize that shortness is no limitation, and even when it is, it is one that can be conquered. (In the case that the shock does not wear off, wrap yourself in a blanket and call an ambulance.)

Shorties on the Big Screen

For the theater one needs long arms; it is better to have them too long than too short. An artiste with short arms can never, never make a fine gesture.—ROLAND BARTHES

Height is an important commodity in the biz. Common wisdom holds that a leading man should be "tall, dark, and handsome," not "short, pasty faced, and weird looking." A leading lady should be "leggy and willowy," not "squat and tree-stumpish." Regardless, many of the best-known actors and actresses in the world have been short. They often try to hide this fact, which has a twofold effect:

1. The exact height of most actors or actresses is always a topic of debate, and is thus difficult to record accurately even in a fine, funny, informative book, or any educational videos that may result from said book.

2. Some of these heights may surprise and tickle you!

ACTORS AND ACTRESSES YOU KNEW WERE SHORT

MICHAEL J. FOX—5'4"—Even though Michael could go *Back to the Future*, he never went to the past and gave himself growth hormones. After starring in the sitcoms *Family Ties* and *Spin City*, Michael became the leading proponent for stem-cell research and finding a cure for Parkinson's disease (with which he is afflicted).

SHIRLEY TEMPLE—5'2"—Perhaps the most famous child star of all time and later a U.S. ambassador to Ghana and Czechoslovakia, Shirley Temple is also the name of a nonalcoholic, cherry-flavored drink. "I'll have a short Shirley Temple on the rocks" might be something a man would say on a first date if he wanted to never have a second date.

MARTIN SHORT—Despite what you might think based on this SNL alum's name, Martin Short is well over nine feet tall.*

PETER DINKLAGE—4'6"—A talented actor, Peter won critical acclaim for his role in *The Station Agent*. He's also frickin' great looking.

NATALIE PORTMAN—5'3"—Do you like Piña Colportmans? That's a parody of the song "Do you like Piña Coladas," using famous movie star Natalie Portman's name.

GILBERT GOTTFRIED—5'5"—If there is a Hell, which there is, the voice screaming in your face all the time will be Gilbert Gottfried's. He voiced the parrot in Disney's *Aladdin* and he swears onstage for a living.

TOM CRUISE—5'7"—Terrifyingly open about love and religion, Cruise is on a Mission Impossible to hide his height from the public. On the other hand, he is so good looking that just being near him causes plants to grow and barren animals to become fertile.

VERNE TROYER—2'8"—By all accounts a towering talent, Verne plays Dr. Evil's compact clone, Mini-me, in the *Austin Powers* movies. He

---

*Just pulling your stunted little leg...Martin Short is 5'6". Here are three more numbers from my credit card: 6, 7, 3.

has breathed new life into the ancient American tradition of Tiny Bald Mike Myers Day.

PETER LORRE—5'4"—One of the all-time weirdest actors, he was in *The Maltese Falcon* and *Casablanca*. He landed his role as the lead in Hitchcock's *The Man Who Knew Too Little* by laughing and nodding —never letting on to Hitchcock that he barely knew English at the time. He then performed the part by learning the lines phonetically.

SEAN ASTIN—5'5"—Sean played Rudy in *Rudy*, an important movie about a short guy who wants to play football for Notre Dame. The lesson of the movie is that even if you are short, as long as you work really, really hard for years and years and years, maybe you can be happy for one second of your life.

ELIJAH WOOD – 5'6"—Sean Astin's costar as a hobbit in *The Lord of the Rings* trilogy. Stoners and nerds everywhere must thank these short men for giving them so much joy and purpose.

WARWICK DAVIS—3'6"—Though not what you'd call "willowy," the British actor played Willow in the movie of the same name, having landed the role through his performance as an Ewok in *The Return of the Jedi*.

BOB HOSKINS—5'4"—Though Bob has been nominated for several Academy Awards, he will be best remembered among shorties for his portrayal of Mario Mario in the *Super Mario Brothers* movie. That, or as some kind of journalist in the movie where John Travolta plays a sexy angel.

HALEY JOEL OSMENT—5'4"—"I...see...short people!" The kid from *The Sixth Sense* is no longer a kid, but he's still a short dude.

SARAH JESSICA PARKER—5'3"—Having danced her way through *Footloose* and tangled with Antonio Banderas in *Miami Rhapsody*, the *Sex and the City* superstar's most surprising role is as the actual wife of real-life international superhunk, Matthew Broderick.

ACTORS AND ACTRESSES YOU THOUGHT MIGHT BE SHORT

In Hollywood if you're good looking, tall, have OK teeth and nice skin, the odds of being successful are great. If you're short and fat, it's a different story. But as long as you look like a leading man type, half your job is done already.—JOHN CORBETT

DAVID SPADE—5'5"—Sarcastically short and senselessly thin, David Spade starred in several popular comedies with his bizarro double, Chris Farley. Spade was romantically linked with Lara Flynn Boyle for a time, only to have her stolen by Jack Nicholson. Suddenly this is a gossip column.

JANEANE GAROFALO—5'1"—Whether you love her or hate her, Janeane Garofalo will not withhold her opinions of you.

PETER FALK—5'6"—The glass-eyed *Columbo* star is also a certified public accountant. As the grandfather in *The Princess Bride,* he keeps Fred Savage's interest by threatening to stop reading at cliffhangers. As a short, myopic man he is wise to leave cliffs well enough alone.

MARILYN MONROE—5'5½"—While she was technically slightly above average height for a woman, I thought it would be worth it to include her for this picture:

JULIANNE MOORE—5'3"—There has maybe never been a movie where Julianne Moore wasn't naked. That said, she has maybe never been in a bad movie.

MIKE MYERS—5'7"—He played Verne Troyer's tall counterpart in *Austin Powers* and Dana Carvey's normal-sized counterpart in *Wayne's World.*

BURGESS MEREDITH—5'5"—Rocky's coach, he was originally supposed to play himself as the love interest, but it sounded too weird when Rocky yelled, "Yo, Meredith! Yo, Burgess Meredith!"

LINDSAY LOHAN—5'4½"—Lindsay was cast as Bette Midler's (5'1") daughter on the short-lived sitcom *Bette*, before switching brains with Jamie Lee Curtis in *Freaky Friday*. Some people think they never switched back...!

JACK BLACK—5'6"—The wacky, tongue-wagging half of the funny-rock band Tenacious D, Jack Black has starred in a number of movies and ruined a bunch of kid's birthday parties by getting out of control. (I assume he did that a lot when he was a kid.)

MAE WEST—5'0"—One of the hottest stars of all time, her petite stature had space for a surprising number of curves. Known as the "Baby Vamp," she was also a provocative playwright.

NORIYUKI (PAT) MORITA—5'3"—Mr. Miyagi in *The Karate Kid* movie franchise. A great supporter of the underdog, Mr. Morita knew how to deal with the short person's propensity for body hair: "Wax on, wax off."

ACTORS AND ACTRESSES YOU NEVER GUESSED WERE SHORT

I act tall!—SALMA HAYEK, 5'2"

LUCY LIU—5'2"—This powerful and beautiful action star tends to wear sky-high heels and is usually matched with short costars, which is why she seems so gigantic.

JENNA JAMESON—5'4"—One of the most famous and successful porn stars. After researching hundreds of her movies, I have determined that she is 5'4" but, trust me, it took a lot of research. One difficulty in determining the height of porn stars is that many of their body parts are wildly out of proportion.

RON JEREMY—5′6″—Case in point: Ron Jeremy, "the Hedgehog," is another extremely famous porn star. I had previously thought he was two feet tall.

JAMES DEAN—5′7½″—This *Rebel Without a Cause* had a cause to be proud of—he achieved film immortality while being slightly shorter than average.

BEN STEIN—5′5″—Ben Stein was a speechwriter for Richard Nixon—but his career took a sharp upswing when he played the monotone teacher in *Ferris Bueller's Day Off*, starring international superhunk Matthew Broderick.

THE SHEENS—Martin Sheen, 5′6″, Charlie Sheen, 5′9″, and Emilio Estevez, 5′5½″—As handsome as they are, it's hard to tell that two-thirds of them are pretty short. Maybe it is because of their huge, disproportionate heads.

ROBERT DOWNEY JR.—5′8″—Thanks to Robert's many run-ins with the law, we know his height from his mug shots.

PENELOPE CRUZ—5′4″—I don't know about you guys, but I'm glad that Penelope Cruz is short.

MARTIN LAWRENCE—5′7″—Martin Lawrence might be short, but his characters are huge!

ACTORS AND ACTRESSES THAT ARE NOT SHORT

KEVIN BACON—5′10″—If the game "Six Degrees of Kevin Bacon" were changed to "Six Inches of Kevin Bacon," I would still be one inch shorter than six inches of Kevin Bacon.

OSCAR WINNERS AND NOTABLE NOMINEES

ROBERTO BENIGNI—5′5″—won Best Actor for *Life is Beautiful*—He was so full of life at the Academy Awards that he was never asked to act again.

DUSTIN HOFFMAN—5'5½"—won Best Actor for both *Kramer vs. Kramer* and *Rain Man*. He has also been nominated for five other Academy Awards for acting, and one more for swimming.

MARY PICKFORD—5'0"—won Best Actress for *Coquette* and an Honorary Award in 1976. In a twenty-seven-year period she made 236 films, but remember that they were easier because they were in black and white.

ELIZABETH TAYLOR—5'2"—won Best Actress for *Butterfield 8* (short and skinny) and *Who's Afraid of Virginia Woolf* (short and chunky), and also received three other nominations and a Humanitarian Award. She is a true legend with her own cosmetics line and a Cleopatra-like ferocity for breaking men's hearts and her own back. (She has had eight husbands and broken her back four times.)

SALLY FIELD—5'2"—won Best Actress for both *Norma Rae* and *Places in the Heart*. Because of her height, she has been able to play both Tom Hanks's mother and his lover (in different movies).

MICKEY ROONEY—5'3"—won a Juvenile Award in 1939 and an Honorary Award in 1983. Known affectionately as "the Mick," he had the longest onscreen adolescence in history, playing Andy Hardy opposite the great **JUDY GARLAND** (5'½")—who won a Juvenile award in 1940. As Dorothy in *The Wizard of Oz*, she befriended many kindred munchkins, and as the victim of some shady MGM practices, also befriended barbiturates and five husbands. In the end, the Mick defeated Judy by marrying *eight* wives and still being alive.

LINDA HUNT—4'9"—won Best Supporting Actress for playing a male dwarf in *The Year of Living Dangerously*. Her height condition and appealingly androgynous facial structure have enabled her to snatch up many other odd roles, as well.

HOLLY HUNTER—5'2"—won Best Actress for *The Piano,* although it was a bittersweet victory, as the actor who played the piano had just died in real life.

AL PACINO—5'6"—won Best Actor for *Scent of a Woman*. He was the star of many great movies, including *The Godfather.* The expression "The shortest guy in the room yells the loudest" was coined by me, about him.

HALLE BERRY—5'5½"—won Best Actress for *Monster's Ball,* and was the first African-American woman to win that honor. Her choices of role are sometimes questionable, but her choice of body is not— short and beautiful.

DAME JUDI DENCH—5'1"—won Best Supporting Actress for *Shakespeare in Love,* a movie in which she appeared for only eight minutes. That means that each inch of her body needed to act for a mere 7.9 seconds!

The Little Screen

NELL CARTER—4'11"—A Tony Award–winning actress and singer, Nell played the wisecracking housekeeper on the sitcom *Gimme a Break*.

JASON ALEXANDER—Perhaps the greatest character actor of his day, Jason Alexander has played everything from George, the 5'5" Larry David–like character on *Seinfeld,* to Jason Alexander, a Jason Alexander-like character on the Larry David show *Curb Your Enthusiasm*.

ESTELLE GETTY AND NANCY WALKER—4'9", 4'11"—The mothers on *The Golden Girls* and *Rhoda*, respectively, these two put the "feisty" in "Oh, those feisty little grandmas."

SUSAN LUCCI—5'1"—Susan has been nominated twenty-one times for a daytime Emmy for her role as Erica Kane in *All My Children,* and finally won for the first and only time in 1999. Maybe they should call her Susan UNlucci!

CARMEN ELECTRA—5'2½"—In 1998, the *Baywatch* star married 6'8" Dennis Rodman in Las Vegas. It is reported that she returned to their hotel room to find Rodman slam-dunking a strange woman, but he immediately explained that the naughty nude had just fallen through the ceiling, which, despite his claims, appeared to be remarkably intact.

DANNY BONADUCE—5'6"—Former member of the Partridge Family and current member of the Alcoholics Anonymous family, the Steroids Anonymous family, and the Crazy Person with a Reality Show family.

Comedy Teams

LOU COSTELLO—5'3"—Played the shorter member of the famous comedy duo Abbott and Costello, whose signature routine was "Who's on First?" Bud Abbott was 5'8". Interestingly, the comedy duo of Stan Laurel and Oliver Hardy also had a five-inch difference in height between them (5'9" and 6'2", respectively). Perhaps that is the "golden ratio" of comedy. (It was previously thought that the golden ratio of comedy was 4.42.)

LARRY FINE, MOE HOWARD, AND JEROME "CURLY" HOWARD—5'4", 5'4", 5'5"—The Three Stooges, Larry, Moe, and Curly, invented the one-handed eye-poke as well as the phrase "Nyuck, nyuck, nyuck." They are beloved by short and tall men everywhere, and by some medium-height women with beards.

HARPO AND CHICO MARX—5'5", 5'4½"—Comedy just keeps getting shorter.

BUSTER KEATON AND HARRY HOUDINI—5'6", 5'4"—Although the two were not technically a comedy team, Houdini co-owned a traveling vaudeville show with Keaton's father, Joe Keaton, when Buster was just a baby. Houdini was one of the greatest escape artists of all time, and he took advantage of the fact that chains and steel vaults were built for much taller men. Buster Keaton was a master of physical comedy who would spend his whole life covered in bruises from daily pratfalls and throwing himself down stairs. (He continued doing painful stunts even into his seventies.)

It's 10:00 P.M. Do You Know How Tall Your Action Stars Are?

Have you ever filmed yourself on a dirt bike, popping a wheelie over your couch, and jumping off to deliver a sweet flying chest kick to your dad? When you watch the movie, does it seem like you are huge and awesome, and your dad is a shriveled husk wishing only for an end to his pain? Or, is it the opposite and you seem like a courageous underdog and your dad is the evil overlord who must be vanquished, or else he will continue to provide for you and the rest of your family? If you answered the latter, then you sent your film to be edited in China. If it is the former, then you probably had your film edited right here in the good ole US of A.

The point I am successfully making is this: while American action movies distort stars' heights by making them seem bigger, Asian action movies make stars seem smaller, so it looks like they are up against tougher odds. (This may be a moot point, since Jet Li is 5'6", Jackie Chan is 5'8", and Bruce Lee was only 5'7½".) In *Fists of Fury*, Bruce Lee is made to seem smaller by having to fight hundreds of huge henchman. On the other end of the spectrum, Arnold Schwarzenegger must face a bunch of cranky kids in *Kindergarten Cop*.

Indeed, American action stars must be tall (even if they aren't really). Schwarzenegger's official height ranges from 6'1" to 6'2". However, some have suggested that he is closer to 5'9" or 5'10", and that not only does he wear lifts and cowboy boots, he also poofs his hair up to gain extra inches.

Movie Tricks

When you're a short actor you stand on apple boxes,
you walk on a ramp. When you're a short star
everybody else walks in a ditch.—MICHAEL J. FOX

Dogg, say what? Actors lie about their heights? Alas, yes. Actors
and actresses lie about their real heights all the time, and
cheat by wearing high heels, platform shoes, and/or lifts in their
shoes, having big hair, or wearing hats that read "I'm tall!" and
shirts that read "Look at my hat." But surely, you say, the camera
doesn't lie! That is where you are wrong, you. Here are some classic
tricks that Hollywood types employ to bilk you out of the hard-
earned money you would only knowingly spend on watching *tall*
actors.

THESE BOOTS WERE MADE FOR ACTING
Actors have been using elevator shoes in movies (and in their personal lives) for years. Bobby Darin, Humphrey Bogart, and even Brad
Pitt have used lifts to give themselves a leg up. An elevator shoe
can have a two-inch lift inside the shoe in addition to a one- or
two-inch heel outside. The problem is keeping your balance.
Another problem might be lying to yourself.

THE "APPLE BOX" DOESN'T FALL FAR FROM THE TREE
"Apple boxes" are stackable boxes used on movie sets for standing on,
sitting on, or placing furniture or cameras on. As long as the camera
doesn't dip below an actor's knees, he or she can stand on an "apple
box" and presto!—taller. Despite what you might think, apple boxes
do not taste like apples, but they are extremely nutritious.

NOT JUST SHORT PEOPLE WEAR ACTIN' BOOTS: **Even the"Duke" himself, John Wayne, wore lifts to add three inches to his already 6'4" frame. Abraham Lincoln didn't wear lifts but he wore a top hat, and legend has it that he had the White House tailor sew him skimpy, ill-fitting suits to make him seem too big even for his own clothes.**

The truth of the matter is that Lincoln wore the top hat because he had a conehead, and his clothes were too tight because he always wore them in the bathtub—he had a phobia of bathwater. This is a fact straight out of the Library of Congress (a fictional library).

CAMERA ANGLES

Using our old friend "perspective," directors can set up shots in such a way that smaller actors appear taller. By positioning shorter actors closer to the camera, they appear larger than their costars in the background. A worm's-eye view makes an actor appear to tower over everything else in the shot. Wide-angle lenses can also distort the relative sizes of objects. Using no camera at all adds yet another level of realism, and using no camera while standing on a ladder above an actor's head makes you feel that you yourself are a security camera.

INCREDIBLE SHRINKING COSTARS

When a leading lady is taller than her leading man, she might be asked to perform barefoot or in thin ballerina slippers, while her costar wears three-inch heels. In the movie *Circle of Friends*, Minnie Driver, who is 5'10", had to walk in a ditch alongside her 5'9" costar, Chris O'Donnell. "The ditch" is not an uncommon practice, but let's just say it's much more pleasant than "the gorge."

TALL ACTORS NEED NOT APPLY

When an important actor doesn't want to deal with lifts and ditches, he can sometimes get a clause in his contract that prohibits the studio from casting anyone taller than he is. One time, General

Motors hired one such actor to work on an assembly line and that is why they had to lay off thousands of tall workers.

JUST MAKE THE WHOLE WORLD SMALLER

In one famous instance, a studio built a set for a western in which one half of the set was smaller than the other. That way, when the short star emerged from a saloon door on the short side of the set, it looked as if he towered over it. Meanwhile, the villains emerged from a much larger doorframe, and thus appeared smaller than the hero. Remember that in America we like our heroes tall, our villains short, and our doorframes varied.

ANIMATION

Superman is actually much shorter than Lois Lane, but animators draw him taller in cartoons and comic books—just another trick of the trade. Likewise, Popeye is over a 150 miles long, but artists typically reduce his size as a courtesy to our mortal grasp of scale.

A RUMOR I'M PRETTY SURE IS TRUE

So he could look into his costars eyes, 5'4" Alan Ladd was filmed only from the shoulders up. What was beneath his shoulders? He was riding a low-flying, magical crop-dusting plane.

MAKE THE WHOLE WORLD SMALLER, YOU SAY...

In 1938, Columbia Pictures put out the movie *The Terror of Tiny Town*, which was a western starring an all proportionate dwarf cast riding Shetland ponies. Since every single thing in the movie was just scaled down, the only noticeable difference from a regular movie was the awful singing and plot. It is considered one of the worst movies of all time. The producer, Jed Buell, wanted to use the cast to make a biopic of the legendary Paul Bunyan, but after the debacle of Tiny Town, the idea fizzled.

Short Sports

L et's face it: with a few exceptions, most popular sports are easier for people with longer and bigger bodies. A short person may be in the best shape, pound for pound, but a taller person's legs will still stride farther, give more leverage, and spin 360 degrees like a crazy upside-down owl. Here are some sweet facts about short athletes who overcame their natural disadvantage to stand head and shoulders above the rest.

BASKETBALL

TYRONE "MUGGSY" BOGUES—5'3"—The shortest player in NBA history, Bogues used his speed and skill to dominate the passing and stealing game for his team, the Charlotte Hornets. In 1993, despite his size, Bogues blocked a shot by 7'0" center Patrick Ewing, with whom he later appeared in the movie *Space Jam* as a basketball player whose skills were stolen by aliens.

DEBBIE BLACK AND TEMEKA JOHNSON—5'3" and 5'3"—The two shortest women in the WNBA are the same height as Muggsy Bogues, and, like him, they both play point guard. Unlike him, they have no connection to the petite gangster Bugsy Mogues.

EARL BOYKINS—5'5"—The second shortest player in NBA history, Boykins is sometimes known as "the Double-Digit Midget." Earl is used to some ribbing about his height. When he played for the Golden State Warriors, his theme music was "It's a Small World." When he played for the Small World Warriors, his theme music was "Mandy" by Barry Manilow.

SPUDD WEBB—5'7"—The shortest player to win the NBA Slam Dunk Contest. Webb learned to dunk before his senior year of high school, when he was only 4'11".

BASEBALL

I'd rather be the shortest player in the Majors than the tallest player in the Minors.—FREDDIE PATEK, 5'4"

"WEE WILLIE" KEELER—5'4"—Played right field from 1892–1910, and had a number of unbroken records, including eight straight seasons with 200 hits or more. Wee Willie's proficiency and frequency at bunting was the driving force for making the rule that calls a third-strike foul bunt an "out." His advice to hitters was "Keep your eye clear, and hit 'em where they ain't"—a wise and pithy statement, but terrible advice for boxers.

"RABBIT" MARANVILLE—5'5"—The leading National League shortstop from 1914 to 1919 (except for 1918 when he was in the navy), Maranville was known for his infield fly-basket catch and for his practical jokes. Always the cutup, on the field he would hand glasses to the umpire, mimic the slow movements of lesser players, or put his cap on sideways and leap into the arms of a bigger teammate. Off the field, he was even wilder, bringing a pet monkey on road trips and having a teammate chase him through Times Square yelling, "Stop Thief!" Legend has it that he even staged his own violent murder, only to walk nonchalantly out of his hotel room after concerned teammates broke down the door.

MARATHON RUNNERS

One would think that people with longer legs would be better at running longer distances, but remember that tall people are weaklings and crooks. In fact, many marathon winners are short for a host of biological and geographic reasons. For example, many good marathon runners are from East Africa (where the high elevation insures their superior lung power), and many East Africans are short.

EDDIE TAKES THE CAKE

On August 19, 1951, the coach of the suffering St. Louis Browns, Bill Veeck, tired of dismal fan attendance, promised one of his team's sponsors that he would do something "no one had seen before" if they would fill the stands with their own advertisers and distributors.

On game day against the Detroit Tigers, there was a big crowd. A large cake was wheeled out to the field, which didn't impress the fans in the least. From the cake emerged 3'7" Eddie Gaedel, a proportionate dwarf in a baseball uniform, carrying a toy bat and wearing the number ⅛ on his back. The crowd had seen it all before and kept moving toward the exit. Only when Gaedel actually approached the plate did people start to pay attention.

The umpire checked the rule book, the catcher lay down behind the plate, and the pitcher did the best he could—but nothing was going to stop Eddie from getting walked. Nothing except Eddie himself. Veeck had shown him how to crouch so that he had absolutely no strike zone but, according to Veeck, Gaedel had "seen DiMaggio too often" and, in imitating his stance, left himself with an inch-and-a-half strike zone, which luckily was small enough to keep him in the box. (It was the smallest strike zone ever in the Major Leagues.) As an added precaution, Veeck told Gaedel, "Don't swing! If you swing, I'm going to be sitting in the press box with a rifle and I'll shoot you right in the head." Gaedel got the walk.

While rules were soon altered to prevent at-bat stunts like this one, Veeck claims that other teams' pitchers started practicing with dwarfs, just in case. Gaedel himself had a rocky personal life, was occasionally hired by Veeck for more publicity, and his autograph now sells for more than Babe Ruth's.

» 103 «

TEGLA LOROUPE—4'11"—Named a United Nations Ambassador for Sport by Kofi Annan in 2006, Tegla holds a number of long-distance world records. Not only was she the first African woman to win the New York City marathon, but she also established annual "Peace Marathons" in wartorn Kenya (her native country), Uganda, and the Sudan, in which world and local leaders run alongside warriors and common folk. Loroupe has become a hero to many Africans, including her 24 brothers and sisters.

JOSIA THUGWANE—5'2"—Josia Thugwane started running marathons as a way to support his impoverished family, only to become the first black South African ever to win an Olympic gold medal, in 1996. Four months before the Olympics, Josia was *shot in the face* by bandits attempting to steal his car. A year after Josia became a national celebrity, he was attacked again: thugs knocked out two of his teeth and hurt his back. Sometimes there is no running away from danger.

A TALE OF TWO FOOTBALLS

SOCCER
Pelé—5'7"—GOOOOOOOOOOOOOOOOOOOAL! Pele is one of the greatest soccer players of all time, and is known as the "King of Football."

FOOTBALL
Barry Sanders—5'7½"—TOOOOOOOOOOOOUCH DOOOOWWWNNN! Barry Sanders is considered one of the greatest running backs of all time and is known as the "King of Soccer."

TENNIS

BILLIE JEAN KING—5'4½"—One of the greatest players of all times and a strong fighter of sexism in sports and in the world, Billie Jean is infamous for defeating the very short and very annoying Bobby Riggs in a high-profile "Battle of the Sexes" tournament.

OLIVER ROCHUS—5'5"—A Belgian, Oliver is the shortest men's professional tennis player ever. He says, "If I am taller, maybe I wouldn't move so well or react to the ball like I do. I don't ever think about my height." A motto to live by.

WEIGHTLIFTERS

Luckily for us, some sports have weight classes.

NAIM SÜLEYMANOGLU—4'11"—The Bulgarian-Turkish "Pocket Hercules" has beaten world records forty-six times and won three Olympic gold medals for weightlifting. He has retired numerous times but has almost always come back to win another championship for the short-with-muscles everywhere. He has twice run for political office in Turkey and twice lost.

YOSHINOBU MIYAKE—5'0"—Japan's greatest featherweight weightlifter and three-time Olympic medalist is known for his powerful "Frog Style."

RACING

Did you know there is a sport in which people just race cars around a track, hundreds upon hundreds of times in a row? Well, there is, and it is called racing. I don't know if it helps to be short to fit into those funny-looking cars, but I do know that **MARIO ANDRETTI, 5'4"**, and **JEFF GORDON, 5'7"**, are two of the greatest race car drivers of all time. Who was the third-greatest? Mother Teresa, 5'0".

OTHER SPORTS

FIGURE SKATING: SCOTT HAMILTON—5'3"—According to Scott, "The only disability in life is a bad attitude." An Olympic gold medalist, Scott suffered a six-year illness as a child that stunted his growth but didn't stop him from doing skating backflips.

BULLFIGHTING: MARIBEL ATIENZAR—5'0"—Olé! Even short people are applauded for taking the lives of innocent bulls.

COWBOY-TYPE STUFF: ANNIE OAKLEY—5′0″—Sharpshooter and main attraction of the Buffalo Bill Wild West show. She could shoot a dime from ninety feet away, or a ninety-foot dime from one foot away. It didn't matter to her, so long as it was a challenge. Her incredible life inspired the musical *Annie Get Your Gun*.

SPEED SKATING: DEREK PARRA—5′4″— Fast at skating. His life inspired the musical *Cats*.

BOXING: JOE WALCOTT—5′1½″—Known as "the Barbados Demon," Joe was a boxer with more muscles than height.

Politics

I heard Dennis Kucinich say in a debate,
"When I'm president... "and I just wanted to
stop him and say, "Dude...."—JON STEWART

Ah, politics, you strange bedfellow—the drug of many idealistic young men and women hoping to make the world a better place. Well, young man, young woman, forget it! Shortness is a crime in American politics—although, unlike some other things politicians indulge in, not one you can go to jail for.

THIS IS HOW PEOPLE THINK POLITICS WORKS

THAT CAN'T BE ACCURATE, CAN IT?

Of all the presidential elections we have held in this country, the taller candidate has won slightly more times than the shorter candidate. Since the 1900s, the taller candidate has had a more statistically significant likelihood of being elected, and since 1950, when television began to take hold, it has indeed gotten harder for shorter candidates to get elected: until 2000, only Richard Nixon and Jimmy Carter had defeated their taller rivals.

Because of our ingrained biases, taller candidates may appear more leader-like, stronger, and more authoritative. However, the

The U.S. Presidents

somewhat superstitious notion that a small height advantage automatically benefits a candidate is beside the point. What is most striking is that there has only been one below-average-height candidate (Michael Dukakis, 5'8") nominated by either party since campaigns started to be televised. It's not whether the taller candidate wins—it's that there haven't been any short ones!

Attention Schoolchildren: This Chart is Accurate

6'4"
(Tallest)

5'11½"

5'6"

Martin
Van Buren

Abraham
Lincoln

William
Taft

U.S. PRESIDENTS AND THEIR OPPONENTS SINCE THE UBIQUITY OF TELEVISION*

1948
Harry S Truman (D) 5′ 9″
Thomas E. Dewey (R) 5′ 8″
Difference 1″

1952
Dwight D. Eisenhower (R) 5′ 10½″
Adlai Stevenson (D) 5′ 10″
Difference ½″

1956
Dwight D. Eisenhower (R) 5′ 10½″
Adlai Stevenson (D) 5′ 10″
Difference ½″

1960
John F. Kennedy (D) 6′ 0″
Richard M. Nixon (R) 5′ 11½″
Difference 0″

1964
Lyndon Johnson (D) 6′ 3″
Barry Goldwater (R) 6′ 0″
Difference 3″

1968
Richard M. Nixon (R) 5′ 11½″
Hubert H. Humphrey (D) 5′ 11½″
Difference 0″

1972
Richard M. Nixon (R) 5′ 11½″
George McGovern (D) 6′ 1″
Difference -1½″

1976
Jimmy Carter (D) 5′ 9″
Gerald R. Ford (R) 6′ 1″
Difference -4″

1980
Ronald Reagan (R) 6′ 1″
Jimmy Carter (D) 5′ 9″
Difference 4″

1984
Ronald Reagan (R) 6′ 1″
Walter F. Mondale (D) 5′ 10″
Difference 3″

1988
George H. W. Bush (R) 6′ 2″
Michael Dukakis (D) 5′ 8″
Difference 6″

1992
William J. Clinton (D) 6′ 2″
George H. W. Bush (R) 6′ 2″
Difference 0″

1996
William J. Clinton (D) 6′ 2″
Robert Dole (R) 6′ 1″
Difference 1″

2000
George W. Bush (R) 5′ 11″
Albert Gore (D) 6′ 1″
Difference -2″

2004
George W. Bush (R) 5′11″
John Kerry (D) 6′4″
Difference -5″

*Winner in bold

The data shows the bleak possibilities for a shorter candidate. Based on the statistical chances of George W. Bush defeating not one but *two* taller candidates, we can only conclude once and for all that he stole both elections.

WORLD WAR II: A TINY CAST OF SHORT CHARACTERS

Hirohito (Showa)—5'5"—Emperor of Japan.

Joseph Stalin—5'6"—Feared and revered Russian Communist leader.

Hitler—5'8"—A bad man.

Franklin Delano Roosevelt—6'2"—U.S. president, quite tall, but wheelchair-bound from polio.

Winston Churchill—5'7"—Wartime prime minister of England.

A fun game you can play at home is to take some of Churchill's most famous and inspiring quotes about the noble efforts of the British in World War II and turn them into funny quotes about being short. Let's try!

"Never in the field of human conflict was so much owed by so many to so few... yes, short people on the whole have certainly contributed the most to human society. Yes."—August 20, 1940

Lady Astor: "Winston, if I were your wife I'd put poison in your coffee."

Winston: "Nancy, if I were your husband I'd drink it."

Lady Astor: "Oh my Winston, you are being very short with me!"

Winston: "I know, right?" [Does a pratfall.]

THERE ARE OTHER IMPORTANT POLITICAL FIGURES IN THE WORLD, YOU KNOW

DAVID BEN-GURION—5'0"—The first Prime Minister of Israel, Ben-Gurion was instrumental in the fight for Israeli statehood. He looked a little bit like Yoda.

MOHANDAS (MAHATMA) GANDHI—5'3"—The greatest non-violent freedom fighter in history campaigned throughout his life for India's independence and for the rights of the lower classes. His height was of no concern to him, as he believed "the strength of the soul grows in proportion as you subdue the flesh."

JOHN HANCOCK—5'4"—This Declaration signer, known for his penmanship, was so short, he had to use the feathers of a bug for his quill.

QUEEN VICTORIA—5'0"—Queen of England from 1837-1901, Victoria was the longest reigning monarch in that nation's history. As the story goes, for every inch of her height, she added another layer of petticoats, thus becoming the only person ever to be wider than she was tall.

MAHMOUD AHMADINEJAD—5'2"-5'6"—Because Amhmadinejad, the President of Iran, is such a controversial figure (antagonistic towards the U.S., possibly developing nuclear bombs, ardently believes that the Holocaust never happened but wishes it had) his height undergoes the same sort of positive and negative fluctuations that Napoleon's and Hitler's did. Many want to portray him as diminutive (which he may be) in order to discredit him, while others argue that he is not so small.

KIM JONG IL—5'2"—The North Korean dictator is 5'2" or 5'3" but he also wears 4-inch elevator shoes. This is without a doubt the least odd of his many eccentricities.

SILVIO BERLUSCONI—5'6½"—The controversial three-time prime minister of Italy has written a book about Napoleon, to whom he feels a strong connection. Perhaps, because of their shared height? Yes.

BARBARA BOXER—4'11"—The junior senator from California is the shortest member of the Senate, and stands on a portable platform known as the "Boxer Box" when she speaks at a lectern. She uses the "Boxer Flask" when things get too slow in subcommittee meetings.

Business People

Since bosses won't give us promotions or raises, we short people have to become our own bosses. It's just like a short person to pull herself up by her bootstraps, jump on a mechanical bull market, and ride it 'til the stocks come crashing up.

ANDREW CARNEGIE—5'0"—Turn-of-the-last-century steel magnate and philanthropist. He invented Carnegie Hall using a peanut.

JACK DANIEL—5'2"—Established the first distillery in the United States. It is unclear whether he personally did not want me to be able to remember college or if it was one of his descendants, but one or the other of them is responsible for what happened on my birthday this year.

ARISTOTLE ONASSIS—5'5"—Multibillionaire who married former first lady Jacqueline Kennedy. He tragically died of old age. Just kidding, it was bronchial pneumonia.

ROSS PEROT—5'7"—Insane billionaire and former insane U.S. presidential candidate. He has huge ears and a heart of gold bullion that is monitored by doctors round the clock, but is *so* worth it.

Criminals

The one noticeable similarity with almost all
serial killer victims is their short height and low weight.
—PAT BROWN, FAMOUS CRIMINAL PROFILER AND TALK SHOW GUEST

Well, I know what some of you are thinking. "Sure, this book is very inspiring for all those squares who want to go into business or acting or emperoring or what-ever, but what if I'm a short delinquent with mayhem on my mind and no moral compass? Aren't there any role models for ME?" Fear not, my miniature riff-raff. There are several boys and girls who are bad to their shrunken bones.

> **DISCLAIMER: If you are easily frightened by terrifying tales of gruesome murders, skip this chapter! To clarify, no murders will be described, but you might get made fun of for being scared. Mwahahahaha! Look away!**

GEORGE "BABY FACE" NELSON—5'4"—A mur-derous gangster in the early 1930s, Baby Face worked with the likes of Al Capone, John Dillinger, Pretty Boy Floyd, and other Depression-era gangsters, although he secretly harbored a grudge against his more notorious

colleagues. Once Dillinger was gunned down, the FBI made Baby Face Public Enemy Number One. It was a dream come true for Nelson, except it was the kind of dream that lasts for two weeks during which you shoot a bunch of cops and then other cops kill you.

BONNIE PARKER—4'10"—Bank robber (with Clyde Barrow). Around at the same time as Baby Face, Bonnie and Clyde terrorized the Southwest, robbing for petty cash and occa-sionally killing people while they did it. A lot of

people thought it was all very romantic. The people who got killed—less so.

CHARLES MANSON—5'2"—This late-'60s psychedelic serial killer had a troubled childhood (legend has it that his prostitute mother sold him for a pitcher of beer) and by the time he was thirty he had spent half of his life in prison for various crimes. When released in 1967 (he paid off the parole board with a pitcher of beer), Manson dreamed of becoming the biggest thing since the Beatles, and set about recording music with Dennis Wilson of the Beach Boys (famous for their song "Surfin' with a Warm Pitcher of Beach Beer"). At the same time, Manson had started to acquire followers who called themselves "the Family." On August 6, 1969, he ordered some of his cult followers to kill whoever was in the former house of a record producer who had rebuffed him (Manson had offered him a pitcher of beer, unsuccessfully). Casualties included movie director Roman Polanski's wife, actress Sharon Tate, who was eight months pregnant (with a pitcher of beer). The following night Manson accompanied his followers to the house of the LaBiancas, a wealthy Los Angeles couple (they owned, like, five pitchers of beer). There, he helped subdue the couple before telling his followers to kill them. The Family is thought to be responsible for some thirty-five murders, and many members, including Charles himself, are in prison for life, with no hope of a pitcher of beer.

Fun side note: one of Manson's followers, Lynette "Squeaky" Fromme (a short nickname if ever there was one), tried to kill President Gerald Ford, purportedly to save the environment. She's in jail, too, but look at the facts: Gerald Ford didn't die for another thirty years after the assassination attempt, and the environment has gotten progressively worse. Just saying.

RUNI TOBER—Very small nineteenth-century Italian robber. Tober's accomplices would smuggle him in a bag into wherever they wanted to steal from, and he would take care of the rest. I once tried to do this using a small dog, but once inside the bank the dog refused to unzip himself from the duffel bag and open the vault for me. God, I loved that dog.

SHORTLIGHT ON... RICHEBOURG: THE SMALLEST SPY IN HISTORY

While in the service of the Duchesse de Orléans (the mother of French king Louis Philippe), during the first French Revolution, Richebourg, 1'11", delivered secret dispatches to royalist supporters by dressing in baby clothes and crossing enemy lines in the arms of a nursemaid. Rebel Frenchmen probably even took a moment to admire that little bundle of innocence, untouched by the horrors of battle. It would have been hard for them to imagine that in those swaddled rags sat a full-grown man transporting spy messages.

Richebourg was fiercely loyal to the Orléans family throughout his life, and from them he received a pension of 3,000 francs a year until his death in 1858, at the age of either eighty or ninety. A spy never tells his age.

This is what it was like when Richebourg was crossing enemy lines (ask any scholar):

SCENE 1.

REVOLUTIONARY 1: Hark! Qui goes there?
NURSEMAID: It is only I, a supple nursemaid, and her ward.
RICHEBOURG [whispers]: Supple? Have you ever even done spy work before?
REVOLUTIONARY 2: Your ward? What exactly does that mean?
REVOLUTIONARY 1 [aside]: Hey man, go easy on her. She said she was "supple."
NURSEMAID: Oh...ha ha, my ward...I am carrying a baby. No time to chat boys, I have to get to...to...
RICHEBOURG [whispers]: To your relative's house!
NURSEMAID: To...the tavern!

REVOLUTIONARY 1: With a baby?
REVOLUTIONARY 2: In the middle of a revolution?
RICHEBOURG: Sacre bleu, what are you saying woman?!
NURSEMAID: What? Oh, ha ha. How silly. I meant, the...the...my baby needs to get to the tavern for...an operation...he's...so...
RICHEBOURG: We're going to die because of you. I can't believe I'm going to die dressed up like a baby.
NURSEMAID: ...he's so...he has rabies. I need to get him home immediately. Thank you, garçons. Merci, merci. Adieu.
[runs off]
REVOLUTIONARY 1: She seemed nice.
REVOLUTIONARY 2: I hope we win this war.

SCENE 2.

[The rebellion is crushed.]

Shorties in Space

U nlike our home planet, space has been kind to shorties. Those NASA space ships are hell for leg room, so smaller people make the perfect astronauts. Maybe once we destroy the Earth and have to move to other galaxies, shortness will become more reproductively advantageous. Anyway, that's the line I use to pick up fast women at bars.

YURI GAGARIN—5'2"—The Russian cosmonaut known as "the Columbus of the Stars" was the first man in space. He was recruited for his physical endurance, strength, and diminutive size. This is where he differs from the Columbus of the Seas, who was recruited because his name was Columbus.

NANCY CURRIE—5'0"—Dr. Currie began working as an engineer at NASA in 1987 and has since gone into space four times for a total of one thousand hours, which really isn't that long when you consider how many hours there have been since time began.

GUS GRISSOM—5'5"—Grissom was the second American in space and the first to go back for a second round. He should've quit while he was ahead: He was killed in the Apollo 1 fire.

Artists

Ars longa, vita brevis. (Art is long, life is short.)
—HIPPOCRATES

Art is an area in which height has almost no bearing. Nonetheless, swapping shoe sizes with these buddies ain't too shabby.

HENRI DE TOULOUSE-LAUTREC—4'11"—Due to a genetic bone condition, Lautrec spent his life painting the lively and bawdy scenes around him rather than participating in them. A fixture at the infamous Moulin Rouge in Paris, Lautrec developed an unmistakable graphic style in his posters and lithographs. He also developed syphilis —so maybe he did participate a little bit.

GREATEST ARTIST IN HISTORY

Have you ever wondered who was the greatest artist of all time? Was it Michelangelo, Leonardo, Picasso, or Duchamp? Well, it was Pablo Picasso, and he was only 5'4". The father of Cubism, who painted *La Guernica* and *Les Mademoiselles d'Avignon*, Picasso was a master of as many art forms as he could reach!

AUGUSTE RODIN—5'4"—One of the greatest figurative sculptors in history. Rodin's bronze masterpieces include *The Thinker* and *The Kiss*, as well as a portrait of our short comrade, Balzac.

JAMES ABBOTT MCNEILL WHISTLER—5'4"—Loved his mother like he loved the roots of abstract painting.

Musicians

If music be the food of love, then it must not be very nutritious,
or else the following geniuses would have been taller.
—WILLIAM SHAKESPEARE

SAMMY DAVIS JR.—5'3"—A member of the famous "Rat Pack" with Frank Sinatra and Dean Martin, Sammy mixed comedy and charm with lounge singing. While Sinatra was known as "Old Blue Eyes," Sammy had only one real eye and enjoyed a less complimentary nickname: "Mr. Little Bones."

GREATEST COMPOSER IN HISTORY

LUDWIG VAN BEETHOVEN—5'4"—Not only was Beethoven short, but he also became deaf, and yet he still composed some of the best sounding and tallest symphonies ever.

PRINCE—5'2"—No matter what name he wants to be called, he's the prince of being short and musical. He once made a man pregnant by making love to a woman near him—that is how potent the dude is.

SHORTABLE QUOTABLES
Boy George, himself a contender for the sexiest man alive, once said: "Prince looks like a dwarf who's been dipped in a bucket of pubic hair." Which begs the question: Don't we all?

LITTLE JIMMY DICKENS—4'11"—This country music legend and hall-of-famer was known for his hits "Take an Old Cold Tater (and Wait)" and "I'm Little but I'm Proud." He referred to himself as "Mighty Mouse in his pajamas."

BOB DYLAN—5'6"—Some scholars believe that Dylan's antiwar anthem "Blowin' in the Wind" was actually about a day when a strong gust knocked him off his little feet and sent him thousands of miles to Vietnam where he could witness the futile atrocities of the war firsthand. Others say that never happened.

DID SOMEONE SAY, "MORE MUSICIANS, PLEASE?"

GUSTAV MAHLER—5'4"—composer
IGOR STRAVINSKY—5'4"—composer
PAUL SIMON—5'3"—singer/songwriter
PAT BENATAR—5'1"—rock singer
PHIL COLLINS—5'5—pop singer
DOLLY PARTON—5'0"—country singer/actress
THOM YORKE—5'4"—lead singer of Radiohead

DO NOT TALK ABOUT JAMES BROWN'S HEIGHT

James Brown, the Godfather of Soul, the Hardest Working Man in Show Business, the Sex Machine, was a short man. He was around 5'6", but you didn't hear that from me. You *definitely* didn't hear that from me, understand?

On January 8, 2007, only days after Brown passed away, Atlanta resident Dan Gulley Jr. shot David James Brooks Jr. twice in the abdomen because of an argument over James Brown's height. In retaliation, Brooks retrieved a gun from his car and fired at Gulley, but he missed. The two then went to the police station, where Gulley confessed.

Just to review the facts. *A man shot another man in the stomach because they had different opinions of how tall James Brown was.* I cannot stress this enough, so please just bear with me for a second: if you tell a person that James Brown was 5'6", and that person thinks that James Brown was a different height, that person might shoot you. Or it is also possible that you, yourself will become so enraged at the other person's idea of how tall James Brown is, that you will lose control and shoot that person.

I am begging you: do not discuss James Brown's height. For the love of God.

Thinkers

No arts, no letters, no society, and which is worst of all,
continual fear and danger of violent death, and the life of man
solitary, poor, nasty, brutish, and short.
—THOMAS HOBBES, *THE LEVIATHAN*, PART 1, CHAPTER 18

When you don't get picked for high school sports teams, you have a lot of time to sit and think. Case in point:

GREATEST PHILOSOPHER IN HISTORY

The eighteenth-century philosopher **IMMANUEL KANT**—5'0"—considered the greatest philosopher in the last five hundred years, probably decided that there should be a universal moral code because of the injustices he had suffered as a short person.

The French philosopher and leader of the Age of Enlightenment, **VOLTAIRE**, 5'3", surely developed his satiric wit as a defense mechanism against the giants of his adopted home, Switzerland.

Writers

Well, I'm about as tall as a shotgun, and just as noisy.
—TRUMAN CAPOTE, 5'4"

Y ou think you have to be tall to write? That is a crazy thing to think—unless, of course, you're thinking you have to write on one of those fourteen-foot novelty typewriters.

HONORÉ DE BALZAC—5'2"—The "Napoleon of the Written Word," Balzac was a French writer in the early nineteenth century who worked fourteen to eighteen hours a day to compile all of his writings into a 150-book collection titled *The Human Comedy*. It is rumored that on his deathbed Balzac would only accept help from Doctor Bianchon. Unfortunately, the doctor was nowhere in sight, since he was a fictional character from *The Human Comedy*.

HARRIET BEECHER STOWE—4'11"—
The daughter of the Reverend Lyman Beecher, Harriet wrote the extremely influential book *Uncle Tom's Cabin*, which, while melodramatic and Christian-salvation heavy, focused on the horrors of slavery and especially the recently ratified Fugitive Slave Act. When she met President Lincoln, it is said that he called her "the little lady who made this big war."

WILLIAM FAULKNER—5'5½"—"The Balzac of the South." One of the greatest American modernist writers, Faulkner aimed to show all of human consciousness through his works, which include *The Sound and the Fury, Absalom! Absalom!* and *A Short Person's Guide to Southern Cooking.*

F. SCOTT FITZGERALD—5'7"—Novelist and screenwriter, Fitzgerald penned *The Great Gatsby*, perhaps to show that small people can achieve "greatness."

JOHN KEATS—5'1"—Though he died very young of consumption, Keats (1795–1821) is known as one of the greatest Romantic poets. Some of his most famous works are "On Looking into Chapman's Homer" and "Ode to a Nightingale." In my research, I have unearthed this lost first draft of Keats's masterpiece "Ode on a Grecian Urn."

ODE ON A GRECIAN URN
By Jonathan "Scoop" Keats
You are so small,
Small like me,
And a bonsai tree.
I do not like Grecian Urns;
They are too flashy,
Plus, what is up with all the naked men?
Just saying.

OTHER AUTHORS:

MARGARET MITCHELL—4'10"—wrote *Gone with the Wind.*
CHARLOTTE BRONTE—4'11"—wrote *Jane Eyre.*
HARLAN ELLISON—5'5"—science fiction writer.
LAURA INGALLS WILDER—4'11"—author of the *Little House on the Prairie* series.

Directors

He's too short, he's too...tall, he's...just not going to work.
—ED WOOD, THE WORST DIRECTOR OF ALL TIME

A lot of movies need directors, and a lot of directors are short, so by the transitive property, a lot of movies need short directors. Some of the best films ever made were directed by short auteurs, including the following:

MEL BROOKS—5'4"

SPIKE LEE—5'5"

MARTIN SCORSESE—5'3"

WOODY ALLEN—5'6"

SCORSESE PARMIGIANA?

When Spanish actor Antonio Banderas was first becoming known in the United States, he had a little trouble with the language barrier. (He learned his lines for 1992's *The Mambo Kings* phonetically, just like our short weirdo brother Peter Lorre did for *The Man Who Knew Too Little*.) According to Banderas, when a reporter asked him what his favorite American foods were he answered, "Francis Ford Coppola and Martin Scorsese!"

Miscellaneous

Here are a few more wildly famous compatriots that you can shop for clothes with:

HARRIET TUBMAN—5′0″—Former slave who helped hundreds of other slaves escape to freedom through the Underground Railroad.

ADMIRAL HORATIO NELSON—5′5½″—Defeated our old friend Napoleon, whilst dying.

DR. RUTH—4′7″—Famous sex psychologist and TV show host. When she was very young, she wrote in her diary, "Nobody is going to want to marry me because I'm short and ugly." She has been married three times—short *is* beautiful, especially if you know a lot of erotic secrets.

MARGARET MEAD—5′0″—Famous social anthropologist who, among other things, studied and compared adolescence in Samoa with adolescence in America. Her discoveries suggested that Americans were whiny prudes compared to the easygoing and open-minded Samoans.

RICHARD SIMMONS—5′4″—Before he was a world-famous peppy exercise guru, Simmons was a 278-pound high school kid selling pralines on a street corner in New Orleans.

BUCKMINSTER FULLER —5′2″—Invented the geodesic dome. In a sphere, no one is taller than anyone else.

Some Miscellany (Bonus)

How Do You Stack Up Against

5'0½"   5'6½"   5'1"   5'7"

Christina Ricci   Gael Garcia Bernal   Bette Midler   Mark "The Fo Hami

These Famous Short People?

5'4"

5'6"

5'0"

Joan
Crawford

Henry
Winkler

Shari
Lewis &
Lambchop

PART FOUR

Suppshort

Livin' la Vida Poca

The name of my condition is Cartilage Hair Syndrome Hypoplasia, but you can just call me Billy.—BILLY BARTY, 3'9"
ACTOR AND FOUNDER OF THE LITTLE PEOPLE OF AMERICA

I want to help you. Not me personally, but I want you to be helped and I want to be the one who takes credit for it. With help, you're going to get a job, find a soul mate, eat right, discover the true path to God, learn some sweet tunes, choose the right camp, buy fine, Italian clothes, and receive the best growth-enhancing hormone treatment that money and emotional and physical pain can buy. How will I do all of this? Mental telepathy. Do you feel it working? I am inside your brain. Creepy, huh?

That was a bust, sorry. On to Plan B. We know that being short puts us at a disadvantage in a lot of areas of everyday life. Most objects, clothes, and edifices are designed with taller people in mind, as are most job and dating opportunities. This section offers some insight into overcoming the many social and physical obstacles we face. If nothing helps, just rest easy knowing that I could be slipping in and out of your mind at any given time.

Shortupations, or Workin' 9 to 5'5"

When someone says, "You've got a great face for radio," they are implying that you are too ugly for TV. When I hear someone with a great set of pipes, I tell them they've "got great height for radio," because so many popular singers are short. Hip-hop and rap, like the blues before them, give rise to nicknames based on physical attributes. The blues had its Blind Lemon Jefferson, while hip-hop had Biggie Smalls (R.I.P.) and Li'l Romeo. Clearly, it's an art form obsessed with categorizing size—and it happens to be dominated by our short brethren. Some examples:

LIL' ZANE COPELAND—5'3"

PHIFE DAWG—5'3"

JERMAINE DUPRI—5'3"

KIMBERLY "LIL' KIM" JONES—4'11"

SISQO—5'5"

BABYFACE (Don't worry about his height—just imagine that he is really tall and has a little baby's face)

Anyhoo, "hip-hop artist" is only one of many professions that are particularly well-suited to short people. Before I tell you what the others are, I need to know more about you. Like any good guidance counselor—which I am not—I will administer a quick personality aptitude test. Sharpen your pencil, eat food off the floor, loosen your tie, take off your blindfold, don't do drugs, fill in the blanks to the best of your ability, and—most important—be honest; this is not a Mad-lib. Begin...now!

I am __ feet and __ inches tall. I am from _____ City, Maryland, USA. I would like to attend the _____ School of Auto Engineering and become a _____ mechanic in my _____'s garage. Thanks for writing this book; it has really helped me with accomplishing all of my dreams. _____ you.

Okay, let's see what you put. two feet, thirteen inches tall; Maryland City, Maryland; The Rabbinical School of Auto Engineering; anger mechanic in your rabbi's garage; and finally...whoa, not cool guys, not cool at all, there are children reading this book.

Anyway, because none of you took this seriously, your results cannot be analyzed. I guess you can just pick whichever of these jobs you like the best, because I really don't care anymore. Good luck. (I'm seriously furious.)

BALL TURRET GUNNER

This was one of the most dangerous jobs during World War II. The ball turret was a small, electrified glass sphere attached to the bottom of a B-17 flying fortress. The gunner had to be short enough to fit upside down in the cramped space for up to seven hours, aiming his two .50 caliber guns at enemy planes, and he had to be strong enough to withstand bullets.

COXSWAIN

The coxswain (pronounced COX-en) is the member of a rowing crew who steers the boat and shouts out commands. Since the coxswain doesn't do any of the rowing, he or she must be very light and able to fit in a tiny seat at the stern of the boat. The coxswain is, in essence, the brain of the boat, just as all short people are, in essence, the brains of society. Need proof? Astrophysicist Stephen Hawking used to be a coxswain. More proof? Everything in our society is run by a centuries-old brain trust comprised of former coxswains and, awkwardly, Stephen Hawking's ex-wife.

CHILD STAR

The actors Gary Coleman and Emmanuel Lewis both played young children on popular television sitcoms well into their teens because of their short stature. Most child stars outgrow their TV roles and turn to new professions—such as shoplifter or ex-child-star—but these two had the grace and genetic complications to stay small and childlike.

JOCKEY

Horseracing is a game of speed, so jockeys need to be small and light, making this the classic career for shorties with sporting aspirations (and no fear). Because maintaining a low weight is so important, many jockeys develop eating disorders. Some even become alcoholics from the stress—and from the long nights staying up drinking with the horses.

Sir Gordon Richards, 4'11", Meets the Queen.

The most successful jockey in history was Willie Shoemaker (4'11"), who, ironically, was paralyzed in a car-accident a year *after* he retired from horse racing (a sport notorious for neck and spinal injuries). In one famous race at Churchill Downs, Shoemaker stood up on his saddle after the sixteenth pole, thinking he had won, not realizing that the track at Churchill Downs has seventeen poles, and thus ended up losing. The same thing would happen three thousand years later, when Willie Shoemaker CCVII would get out of his space ship on Jupiter, not realizing the space race went all the way to Saturn. Win some, lose some, yet-unborn Willie Shoemaker CCVII.

GYMNAST

Shorter gymnasts can often outperform taller competitors, because their narrower waists can rotate more quickly during moves, which allows them to do more complex, explosive routines. For this reason, coaches recruit children in the bottom thirtieth percentile of height, figuring that it isn't worth training a child intensively for years if he or she is going to grow to 6'5".

> **THE BEST GYMNASTIC COUPLE: NADIA COMANECI AND BART CONNER**
>
> Nadia, a 4'11" Romanian, was the first-ever gymnast to receive perfect 10s for her performances in the Olympics. Her husband, Bart, 5'6", has won more gold medals than has any other American male gymnast. Together, they are exactly 10'5".

Due to the rigorous training and dietary regimen of gymnastics, puberty is very often delayed, which is why the legal drinking age for gymnasts is forty-three.

BOGGLE CHAMPION

There is no statistical correlation that proves shorter people are better at Boggle, but I happen to be the best Boggle player I know, and I'm pretty short. And handsome.

> **JOBS THAT ARE CERTAINLY NOT SUITABLE FOR SHORT PEOPLE**
>
> Basketball player
> Giraffe groomer
> Lightbulb changer
> Elephant barber
>
> Coconut picker
> Lice checker
> Ladder
> Norwegian

"Looking Up" to People in Social Settings

Come down, o maid, from yonder mountain height:
what pleasure lives in height?—ALFRED, LORD TENNYSON

You know what it's like: you're at a cocktail party, standing in the corner near the chips and diet soda, looking at a sculpture that you later find out is just part of a broken bowl of onion dip that never got cleaned up, and suddenly you have an urge to socialize. For whatever reason—you're lonely, you want to find love, you want to make a business connection, you forgot your house keys and want to borrow someone else's, you remembered something really interesting about your family that you want to tell a stranger, you thought of a really clever pun, you just realized that the perfect last word for the novel *The Brothers Karamazov* would have been "smellsville"—whatever the reason, you need to talk to someone. No matter how you rationalize it, it's miserable to be short in that situation.

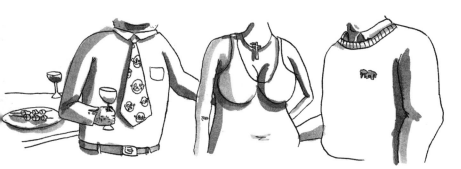

What We See

Look, it's not like we think about our height 24/7. Sometimes hours go by when I don't even realize that I'm very short—after all, when I'm alone, I'm the tallest person around—but when I'm in a social setting, surrounded by clumps of tall people, I get pretty tired of staring at their Mickey Mouse ties and Minnie Mouse belt buckles.

SOCIAL SHORTNESS, A PLAY IN ONE ACT

THE SCENE: *A cocktail party during the holiday season. Guests are numerous, mingling, and still arriving. Booze flows freely, but at the end of the night you have to pay your tab. That's how tabs work. It's not really free. Keep your wits about you, junior.*

A short man named Tom is standing by the punch, looking at his reflection in the ladle to see if there are any ants-on-a-log stuck in his teeth.

MAURICE: Mind if I cut in, stranger?

TOM: Pardon?

MAURICE: Looks like you and that punch ladle are in the middle of something. I don't mean to interrupt.

TOM [confused]: Um, no. Just getting some punch.

MAURICE [punches Tom lightly on the shoulder]: How's that for punch, huh?

TOM: Heh, yeah.

MAURICE: Merry Christmas friend, put 'er there.

TOM: Okay...ungh. [winces in pain]

MAURICE: How'd'ya like that handshake, little fella? I call that the Texas Terror, because I'm from Texas. Jesus, your hand is like a tiny baby's hand. It's like your hand just came up out of yer mama's belly.

TOM: Well, it didn't.

MAURICE: But you see what I'm saying though. Hey, Margie! Come on over and feel this little guy's hand!

MARGIE: How fun! Little man, show me your hand!

TOM: I'd really better be going.

MAURICE: They don't like to be called little, Margie, they's vertical challenged, like those pygmy horses what we rode in South America.

MARGIE: How precious! Clancy, Beauregard, Volpe, Chrysanthemum! You must come over and meet our new friend!

CLANCY: Splendid!

BEAUREGARD: Splendide!

VOLPE: Good gracious, he's darling!

CHRYSANTHEMUM: Splendido! Where ever did you get him?

MAURICE: Just found 'im. Hey, how're everybody's stocks doing?

CLANCY: Can't complain, you know.

BEAUREGARD [sotto voce]: He means he can't physically complain. You know, what with the recent face transplant. He can't frown or his face will reject itself.

TOM [too short to hear the conversation]: What?

VOLPE: I'm sorry, but we can't look down every time we say something, young man.

TOM: I'm forty-four years old.

VOLPE: What was that? Ouch, there it goes again, my neck.

CLANCY: You're upsetting me, Volpe, and I really shouldn't get upset. My face.

MARGIE: I just noticed that the little fellow is staring right at Chrysanthemum's breasts.

CHRYSANTHEMUM: How darling!

TOM: I'm not staring! That's just where my eye level is.

MAURICE: How's the weather down there?

TOM: It's the same as up there. I'm about four inches shorter than you.

MAURICE: Cloudy?

[*End Scene*]

Did you catch all of that? In that one dramatic recreation, we touched on the main factors that make socializing so difficult for short people.

HANDSHAKE: Taller people have bigger hands. They use these big hands to crush short people's hands. Short people, here is what you must do: when shaking hands, grab the other person's hand a split-second too soon, so that you're squeezing the base of his fingers. Do you know what you have just done? You have hurt your father-in-law's hand. Do you know what else you have done? You have earned his respect.

EYE CONTACT: Short people often have to look up when they are talking. It makes your neck hurt, it is awkward, and more often than not it means you have to take a step or two back in a crowded place just to be at a reasonable angle and not nestled in the crook of some tall stranger's neck or armpit. There's no real solution to this problem. Oh wait, there is *one* solution:

THE "KID" SYNDROME: Because growth is a tangible mark of adulthood, people often treat short people like children. Because tall people find it cute, short people will sometimes act babyish around them. You see where I'm going with this—suddenly everyone under 5'7" is a mewling infant and society comes to a standstill. That is how important this stuff is. *Even the stuff that is made up.*

TOPICS OF CONVERSATION
Here are some things people like talking about:

Things they know about.
Things that are going well for them.
Movies they have seen and have strong opinions about.
Food they ate that was good or bad.
The weather. How it is changing. How it is staying the same.
Where they live. Where they used to live. What is nice about places they either live or used to live.
Some people like to talk about sports that they watch regularly.

Here are things people do not like talking about:
Their insecurities.
Bad smells.
Animals who vomit.
Things you want them to do for you.

Short Dating

At 34 she is an extremely beautiful woman, lavishly endowed by
nature with a few flaws in the masterpiece: She has an insipid
double chin, her legs are too short and she has a slight potbelly.
She has a wonderful bosom, though.—RICHARD BURTON

Dating is hard for everyone, whether you're short or tall, fat or
thin, pizza or pasta, or ice-cream. Sure, some people seem as
if they don't have any trouble dating, but it's important to realize
that when those seemingly happy people go home to their duplex
penthouses, lie down on their round waterbeds with bearskin blan-
kets and sharkskin pillowcases, and have meaningless, sensuous,
unbelievable sex with someone they know only from having seen her
picture in a fashion magazine or Hollywood movie, yes, when they
do all that, okay, I sort of lost my train of thought.

So, except for a few people, everyone has trouble dating. Short
people have more trouble, due in part to the fact that we learned
in Part 2: women are attracted to taller men. Some studies have
shown that less than 15 percent of women in the United States are
willing to date a shorter man, and the woman is shorter in almost
99 percent of heterosexual marriages. (In homosexual partnerships,
these statistics are more encouraging: the man is almost always
shorter than the man and the woman is nearly always shorter than
the woman.) Those are pretty rough odds if you are a short man.
Online dating sites and personal ads invariably ask about height,
and some sites won't even permit a shorter man to ask out a taller
woman, regardless of any other characteristics.

Now, I'm not here to preach. If women are attracted to taller
men, then so be it, we are all slaves to our pheromones. But peo-

ple find other people attractive for a whole host of crazy reasons, and height is only one of them. If you feel hindered in dating because of your height, that's a bummer, but a winning personality, kindness, and some sexy hair go a long way. And confidence. Be as confident as if you were tall. Don't get embarrassed about your height. Achieve your goals. You can have your cake and eat it, too. Dip a frog in a frying pan and call it the declaration of independence. Marry a unicorn. The world is your oyster, so tickle it.

PICKING UP STRANGERS

It's hard to be confident when you don't know what to say. Here are some good ways to start a conversation with a tall stranger:

"Why hello there, I didn't realize the ceilings in this place were so low. Do you want to come back to my place and find out about the floor?"

"I've never met a woman quite so enchanting. You're like a tree trunk and I'm a little otter."

"I think height is just a frame of mind. My frame of mind is very short."

"I may be short, but my family has a history of longevity."

"I may need a ladder to kiss you, but I'm willing to go get one."

"I don't know about you, but I'd like to get out of here and find out more about the differences in our bodies."

"I saw you from across the bar and I couldn't help but notice how much you were pointing and giggling about how short I am."

WHAT IF I'M ALREADY DATING SOMEONE TALL?

George: You know what I'd like to do? I'd really like to have sex with a tall woman. I mean really tall, like a giant, like six foot five.
Jerry: Really?
George: What was the tallest woman you slept with?
Jerry: I don't know, six foot three.

George: Wow! Oh my god! See this is all I think about—sleeping with a giant. It's my life's ambition. —Seinfeld

Instead of telling you how to snag a tall lady or grab at a hunk of man, let's assume you've somehow managed to charm the pants off a giant and now you're having logistical problems with the height gap. Here are some pointers:

Problem	What to do if you're the short person	What to do if you're the tall person
Dancing	Twist your ankle and suggest a movie.	Laugh and insist on breakdancing—which involves no contact.
Someone makes a mean comment	Don't let it bother you, and start smooching in public to make them jealous.	Smooch.
The three-legged race at the company picnic	You shouldn't be dating someone at work anyway—office policy.	Use your short mate as your third leg.

SOME OTHER SOCIAL CONFIDENCE TIPS

If you don't think of yourself as short, other people will be less likely to categorize you that way. Some natural ways to make people forget you are short:

LIFT WEIGHTS AND EXERCISE: People will see you as strong before they see you as short.

GROW A HUGE AFRO. When Anna Swan was working for the circus, she was accurately billed at 8'0" because she wore her hair high.

ALWAYS HOLD YOUR ARMS STRAIGHT UP, bend your elbows, and lock your hands right above your head. This will look like you are resting an extra, invisible head in your hands, and people will start to think you are as tall as your invisible head.

ALWAYS WEAR A CAPE AND CARRY A CANE. Instead of people thinking you are short, they will just think you are a duke.

FACE FACTS: leave dating to the pros.

Dancing Short

"Not for me a tall and dandy captain with a shaven chin,
flaunting all affectedly his dainty lovelocks as he struts;
I'd prefer one short and band-legged , with a heart within
stout and good, and firmly planted on his feet, and
full of guts." —ARCHILOCHUS, 7TH C. GREEK POET

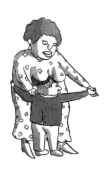

Most dances are not
designed for short
people. Case in point:

Here are some dances that are more suitable.

Personals

A short saying oft contains much wisdom.—SOPHOCLES

Tall SWF looking for an R2D2 to my C3PO.

Short, ladderless, apple-farming lady looking for a tall man to pick apples.

Short man crawling through desert looking for water.

Tall oasis in desert looking for tall man to shower with water and fruit. No short men please!

Short elephant looking for tall pig.

I am a tall man who likes the finer things in life. Long walks on the beach, short walks on the beach, brief naps on the beach, and extended napping and eating on the beach. If you are a short woman who doesn't mind being homeless on the beach, give me a call...in a seashell.

Tall sea captain seeks short first mate. No crybabies.

Tallish woman seeks smallish woman for mediumish commitment.

Fat man on diet looking for short stack of pancakes.

Short stack of female pancakes looking for the fat man who ate her husband.

Short lumberjack looking for tall trees.

Dining Short

If I were overweight because I ate too much I would have far more of a complex. I would know if I just stopped eating and showed a little discipline I would be thin. But there's not a hell of a lot I can do about being short. You just gotta run with it.
—MICHAEL J. FOX

You've done the unthinkable by making friends of all sizes and getting invited to dinner at the house of a delightful and attractive acquaintance. You arrive with flowers and a box of candied yams—classy. You stare lovingly and lustily into the deep pools of his or her eyes, you slowly sit down together, and WHOOMP! Your chair is the wrong size completely. Your chin is practically resting on the table while your feet are dangling in midair like the limp, superfluous limbs of a ventriloquist's dummy trying to dance.

Once you are finally sitting at a reasonable height, there are other problems. How do you know which utensils to use—should you only use the small ones because you are small, or should you use the big ones to compensate for shorter arms? Etiquette dictates that you start a meal using the smallest utensils, which are on the outermost ends of your place setting, and work your way in toward those big ones. Use your oyster fork, which is the smallest and outermost one, then, move on to your fish fork, which is the second shortest. Then put your napkin on the table and say that you're really not hungry anymore because you had a big lunch. Since all well-mannered people believe that the meal is over only when the host or hostess puts his or her napkin on the table, your hosts will become disoriented and think they are the guests. They will promptly thank you and leave their house, providing you with a lovely, new, furnished home.

ADJUSTABLE CHAIR HEIGHT TIP

Here's what to do when you find yourself seated in a chair that is far too high. Talk very expressively, making big sweeping gestures, until you manage to knock your napkin and silverware on the floor. Do this several times in a row. People will always give you new napkins and silverware. When you reach down to pick up your cutlery, quickly stack the knives, forks (tines facing down), and spoons on your

chair in a log-cabin arrangement (see diagram). Cover the whole stack with your napkin. After four or five "accidents," you'll be as tall as the queen of England!

Fig. 1

Tines
Down

Fig. 2

Fig. 3

Welcome to Short Camp

The "Fat Camp" craze is booming in the United States and I'm a little envious. I would much prefer running around, playing games, swimming in a lake, and eating light summer fare to how I spend summers now that I'm an adult—at work in a coal mine data accumulation center three hundred feet underground. I don't even receive benefits. Or a salary.

Now just imagine a place called "Short Camp." It would be similar to a fat camp, because we all have a much better chance of reaching our full height potential if we eat right and exercise. But there would be a lot of awesome activities geared toward the short.

SHORT CAMP DAILY SCHEDULE

5:00 A.M.: Wake up happy.

5:01 A.M.: Get dressed in short clothes!

5:05 A.M.: Clean the bunk.

5:30 A.M.: Stretch for three hours (stretching might make you taller).

8:30 A.M.: Breakfast.

9:00 A.M.: Sit upright in a chair for four hours (better posture can add up to two inches).

1:00 P.M.: Lunchtime.

1:30 P.M.: Naptime (growth occurs when we're sleeping—even if it's only water growth).

5:00 P.M.: Sports—(volleyball on the tennis court, tennis on a Ping-Pong table, baseball on a maple leaf, soccer in a cage).

10:00 P.M.: Dinner.

11:00 A.M.: Accounting class.

1:00 A.M.: Bedtime.

I know it seems a little Spartan, but it's a lot better than it used to be in the old days. This daily schedule from Camp Tiny Teens, a little known Catskills getaway in the '50s, is a grim reminder of what being short used to be like in this country.

CAMP TINY TEENS DAILY SCHEDULE

5:00 A.M.: Wake up.

5:30 A.M.: Get dressed.

5:01 A.M.: Calisthenics and push-ups.

6:00 A.M.: Eight hours in "the box."

2:00 P.M.: Breakfast—gruel.

3:00 P.M.: Lunch—reheated gruel.

3:30 P.M.: Dinner—leftover cold gruel from breakfast.

5:00 P.M.: Five hours in "the box."

10:00 P.M.: John Birch Society meeting.

12:00 A.M.: Group denunciations.

3:00 A.M.: Lights out.

Short Person's National Anthem

TO THE TUNE OF
"MY COUNTRY 'TIS OF THEE"

My country is mini,
My head and bones are tiny,
Of thee I sing.

Land where the forks are short,
Land where the homes are short,
From e-e-every mole-hillside,
Everything is short.

Land where the clothes are short,
Land where the schools are short,
From e-e-every mole-hillside,
Many things are short.

Land where the cars are small,
Land where the mountains are small,
Land where the restaurants are small,
Land where the malls are strip malls,
Land where the strip clubs are just clubs,
Land where our ears are small,
Land where our beers are tall,
Land where the tub is small,
Land where our cubs are small,
Land where the mice seem large,
Land where our pants fit right,

Land where other pants are snug,
Even our rugs are small,
Even the largest kind of rug is small,
From e-e-every mole-hillside,
Everything in the land of the small is shortish.

(gospel choir joins in)

Land where the mirrors are small,
Land where the reflections in the mirrors are small,
Land where the reflections from a small lake are small,
Land where the reflections we make in our minds are small,
Though our minds are not small,
Even if our brains physically are small,
Because our heads are small,
Because our bodies are short,
From e-e-every mole-hillside,
Even our metaphors are proportional.

Land where we're happy to be short,
And everyone is happy for us to be short,
Because they are also short,
Since that's the norm around here,
Although, then what is considered short,
If everyone is short then who is comparatively short,
From e-e-every mole-hillside,
There are questions within questions in the land of the short.

My country is mini,
Like my friends and family,
We are all short.

Praying Short

Young man—your arm's too short to box with God.
—JAMES WELDON JOHNSON, NOVELIST AND POET

What gives life meaning? Is it writing a poem, composing a song, or painting a picture? For me, it is sipping wine on my veranda, staring at all the beautiful women who walk past, and begging them for money. For religious people, it is worshipping stuff or a guy or a lady, or several guys or ladies. But let's get down to it: As a short person, which religion is right for you?

GODS

Thinking about becoming a **HINDU**? In his fifth avatar, Vamana, the Hindu god Vishnu takes on the form of a dwarfish Brahmin in order to fool the demon king Bali. If you are the kind of person who doesn't want to worship a god who is taller than you are, then you might want to become one-fifth Hindu.

> JESUS was 5'1". That's a known fact.
>
> Speaking of biblical shortness, the shortest passage in the New Testament is "Jesus wept" (John 11:35), which refers to Jesus weeping over Lazarus's tomb. The longest passage is when Jesus goes shopping.
>
> In the CHRISTIAN New Testament, Jesus dines at the house of the chief of the Publicans, a dwarf named Zacchaeus. They ordered Thai food.

RASTAFARIANS believe that the Messiah was Haile Selassie I, the 5'4" emperor of Ethiopia from 1930 to 1974. As a politician, Selassie had his ups and downs, but he's allowed more leeway as a deity.

If you like old religions, perhaps you would like to worship Bes, the fat, fun-loving, feisty, dwarf god of the EGYPTIANS.

> **If you hate old religions, start a new one! You will need:**
>
> Some crystals.
> Some incense.
> Pita chips and hummus.
> Some gullible, possibly crazy friends.

PROPHETS

Joseph Smith, the founder of MORMONISM, claimed that the people who lived on the moon were all uniformly six feet tall, wore Quaker clothes, and lived up to one thousand years. (Save for this last detail, he was basically describing himself.) That shouldn't really affect your decision to become a Mormon, but don't try to join the sect that lives on the moon because you will stick out like a sore moon-thumb.

The **MUSLIM** prophet Muhammad was neither tall nor short, so maybe that's a selling point for you. According to some texts, Muhammad said that Adam (of Adam-and-Eve fame) was sixty cubits tall, which is about ninety feet. The hardest-working man in Eden? Adam's tailor.

SAINTS

The **ROMAN CATHOLIC** Saint Joan of Arc was 4'11" and seventeen years old when she led the French army against the British in the early fifteenth century. Burned at the stake as a heretic, Joan was found innocent of heresy some twenty-five years after her execution, which must have come as a huge relief to her.

ACCOMMODATIONS

In 2005, archaeologists dug up the world's smallest temple in the southern rim of the Taklimakan Desert in northwest China. The 1,500-year-old Mahayana **BUDDHIST** temple is 7.4 feet long and 4.25 feet tall, which leaves room only for a pretty short congregation.

In 2007, in Newton, Massachusetts, a cleaning woman found a shrine to some Victoria's Secret catalogues, a 1993 *Sports Illustrated* Swimsuit Edition, and one yellowed copy of *Mrs. Dalloway*, by Virginia Woolf. The shrine is believed to belong to a man no taller than 5'3", based on class photos found nearby. Saint or sinner? That is for the god of short people to decide. (The god of short people is a cat who plays the piano.)

SACRED TEXTS

Author Arundhati Roy wrote a book called *The God of Small Things*.

Growth Procedures

If you persist in believing that it is glamorous to be tall, you are probably thinking, if only there were some horrible, inhuman way of making myself taller...

Leg Lengthening

Cosmetic leg lengthening used to be primarily for children with legs of uneven length or for people with dwarfism, but nowadays the procedure is open to more of the short community (as well as Ethan Hawke's character in the movie *Gattaca*).

The operation consists of four parts:

First, you consult with a doctor who x-rays your legs. Even a moron can do this part. I've done this like a hundred billion times.

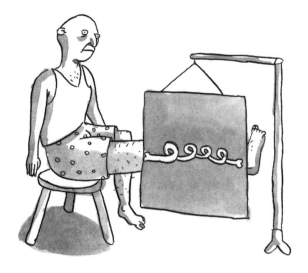

In phase 2, you undergo "surgery" in which a "doctor" breaks the tibia and/or fibula bones of your lower leg. Steel pins are shoved through the bones and attached to an external fixator device with screws.

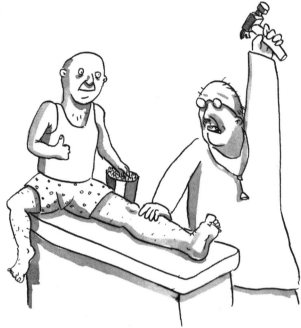

During the "lengthening" phase you are wheelchair-bound and the screws attached to the fixator device are turned, separating your bones by no more than 1 mm per day. This part hurts SO MUCH that it requires A LOT OF PAIN MEDICATION for all of the PAIN. As the bones are separated, new bone tissue grows in the spaces, producing two to three inches' more leg over a period of two to three months.

The last phase is known as the "strengthening" phase, which can last from three months to a year. The external frame is removed and you undergo physical therapy but you are not allowed to walk until the soft bone is able to withstand your weight. At the end of it all, you will be several inches taller and, as a special bonus, using your new legs you will be able to predict when you are going to need more pain medication.

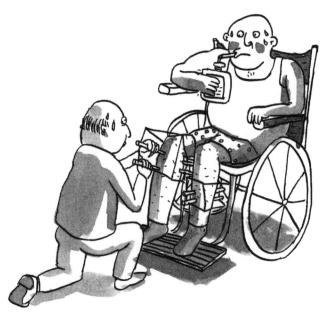

BEFORE   AFTER

Since it began to participate more actively in global trade and business, China has unofficially set height requirements for diplomatic and government jobs, typically 5'2" for women, and 5'7" for men. There are requirements for health and appearance as well. For instance, in Hunan Province, to receive a government job, women have to show that they have symmetrical breasts. Imagine passing all of the height requirements and then getting nailed on the breast symmetry exam. When will people just learn to go through puberty correctly?

Growth Hormone Treatment

Growth hormone treatment is a powerful tool in helping people with growth hormone deficiency to reach their full height potential. How does it work? This may get a little scientific for a second, so I suggest you turn up your radio while you read so there's a soundtrack and it seems like you're studying for "the big test" in a movie about medical school.

As we learned in the introduction, endocrine problems can cause growth failure. The pituitary gland (a tiny but very important gland in your brain) produces a hormone called *somatotropin* (or growth hormone, or GH), which is responsible for making your skeleton grow.

TONGUE TWISTERS

Try saying the following words 10 times fast:

1. Somatotropin   2. Pituitary   3. Mathfart

Human growth hormone treatment creates somatropin for you (somatropin is biosynthetic somatotropin—go figure, right?). It comes in powder form and is mixed and injected into growth deficient children daily, with almost immediate results, including vertical growth as well as increased muscle strength, bone density, and fat loss.

> ### LITTLE SOMATOTROPIN OF HORRORS
> **The first human growth hormone treatments were performed in the 1950s, and the hormones were retrieved from pituitary glands of cadavers, which could pass on diseases to the recipient.**

GET YOUR KIDS CHECKED OUT

The earlier that a growth hormone deficiency is detected, the more chance your kid has of growing to his or her full height. Are you a bad parent if you didn't get your kid checked out early on? Heck, no. Being short is the best. However, now that you know, go get that kid some hormones. If you are a kid and you are short and reading this, go to bed! Wait, no, brush your teeth first. Then, go to bed!

Okay, it's not all synthetic puppies and lollipops. Synthetic GH can cost up to $1,000 a week, and it is important that it be given only to children who are not producing enough growth hormone already.

WHAT ELSE IS BAD?

What's bad? Juicin' is bad! Using synthetic human growth hormone in combination with anabolic steroids is juicin'—which is bad! A lot of professional athletes started doing this in the '90s because of the increased muscle mass and strength that HGH gives, and because it is so hard to detect. But using steroids is cheating. It would be like if, instead of spell check, there was a tool that made your writing more evocative and poignant, or if, for writing poetry, instead of a rhyming dictionary; there was some kind of pastoral metaphor dictionary. Did *that* finally get through your thick athlete skulls, juicers? Good. Now go work out for ten hours a day for thirty years.

I was really short. I remember going to the doctor to see if there were injections I could take to be taller. But whenever we ran a lap, I wanted to run the fastest. I don't know why, on the wheel of fortune of personality traits, it stopped on ambition and hustle and drive.— Proof that Lord of the Rings *and* Rudy *star Sean Astin takes steroids for acting*

Less Severe Methods of Height Increase

STILTS: Stilts are actually sort of hard to use. A lot of people don't know that.

THE OL' BRICK-IN-SHOE: Wear a shoe with a brick on or in it. Pretty simple. You'll be shorter when you're barefoot at the beach, but if that doesn't bother you, then go to the beach. Quickly! Our beaches are eroding.

FOOT WORKOUTS: If you got enough muscle in the bottoms of your feet, you could probably pull off another nine or ten inches.

STRETCHING: Stretching twice a day can improve your posture, which makes a huge difference in height. Stretching will also make you more limber, which is important for your blossoming career in modern dance.

Object Shrinkers

Not only can science make short people taller, but it can make tall objects smaller. There are a number of inventions that accommodate the short way of life (e.g., smoking cigarillos and sipping caviar milkshakes in a Ford minibus).

CARS: Some manufacturers make cars that are smaller for short people, while others sell products that make driving in a standard-size car easier. These include brake and pedal extenders, cushions, and even artificial floors. I never thought I'd say this, but with all those fancy accessories, I wish...I wish I was a car.

CARBAGS: A scary thing about cars for short people is that airbags can crush a short person's face. In accidents, airbags fly out at 200 mph in order to stop you from hitting the steering wheel, but if you are short and sitting close to the wheel, the airbag will hit you so hard it might fracture your skull, break your bones, snap your neck, sleep with your wife, or tell your kids dirty limericks about their grandma. Science's solution? Disable your airbag. Now you have a choice of which automotive way you want to die.

UNMENTIONABLES: There is lingerie for short people. I don't want to talk about how I know this, but let's just say it is expensive.

TENNIS RACKETS: Five-foot-nine tennis star Michael Chang realized that he needed a longer racket to compensate for his stature and wingspan, and thus the twenty-eight-inch racket was born (an inch longer than standard). The effect? It was like giving a car to someone lagging in a foot race and allowing him to use that car for the purpose of racing.

SUBWAYS: No, they don't make mini subways for small people, although that would be very cute. Instead, in February 2007, the

Washington D.C. Metro installed spring-loaded overhead handlebars in their commuter cars so that short people who are standing will have something to hang onto. This was preferable to their first idea: installing tall men with spring-loaded handlebar mustaches.

HOUSES: A house that is all small? Yes.

HORSES: They make small horses. They're called ponies.

A RANT ABOUT CLOTHES

I'm a man, but when I put on a man's size medium T-shirt it looks like a muumuu. Pants that fit my waist go below my shoes. When I put on a dress shirt that fits my neck, I have to tuck so much of it into my pants that it looks like I'm wearing a diaper. If you are a short girl, no need to shell out big money for a wedding dress with a long train, as any normal dress will do. Likewise a man can just cut a seam in the back of a regular tuxedo coat and he'll have a nice set of tails. A hat? Why not wear a glove on your head? Sunglasses? Bottlecaps should fit. You get the point. They should make clothes that fit short people.

Non-Growth-Enhanced Coping

As a kid I was short and only weighed 95 pounds.
And though I was active in a lot of sports and got along
with most of the guys, I think I used comedy as a defense
mechanism. You know making someone laugh is a much better
way to solve a problem than by using your fists.—TIM CONWAY

Everyone only gets one chance at life, and we all have to choose how we want to spend that one shot. If you are short and you're not planning to get your legs lengthened, then you are going to be short no matter how hard you try or strive or think or cry. What you can control is how you deal with it.

Saying the world isn't fair won't make it any more so. Taking yourself too seriously will only get you laughed at more. Starving yourself will only make you too thin and gorging yourself will only make you too happy.

As corny as it seems, having a sense of humor about your height will help you stop thinking of it as a drawback, and other people will follow your lead. And anyway, if shortness is the worst thing you have to deal with, then consider yourself very, very lucky. At least you weren't born like this:

So look on the bright side:

ADVANTAGES OF BEING SHORT

You can reach things low to the ground.
You can fit in small spaces.
You can stretch out on couches that other people get squished on.
You can make a blanket out of a sweatshirt.
You can make a sweatshirt out of two dirty socks and an umbrella.
Tall people are happier for you when you something goes your way and they don't even know why.
Although it may be worse when you're in the back row at a concert, you can always push through to the front and no one will mind.
You don't have to bend down in field hockey.
You're less at risk of a heart attack (according to some studies).
Animals fear you (really small ones, that is).
You don't have to use one of those pesky airbags.
Pools and shallow lakes are more exciting.
No one looks up into your nostrils unless you pay them to.
A lot of people like you.
You're nice.
You can ride a turtle.

What My Life Would Be Like If I Were Tall

Let's step back for a second, out of our proscribed roles. I won't be the author of this book and you won't be the reader. In fact, to really get into this exercise, I'm going to give you some space to write while I go back a few chapters and reread some of my favorite jokes.

Now that we've let down some of our defenses, I think we can be honest with each other and admit that, sure, we'd like to be tall.

Or at the very least, we'd like to know what it's like to be tall—and for that reason I will provide you with my pretty good guess of what indeed that is like.

> *I wake up. My feet are oddly cold. Ah, yes, my legs are longer than my bed so my feet hang over the sides. This is the price I pay. I look over at my grandfather clock and realize that I am almost late for work as a business executive/amateur basketball star. Quick, what should I wear? My butler brings me the newspaper and some scrambled eggs as I drive around my drive-in closet. A big problem I have is that when I go to a store, everything fits me so well that I just can't resist buying many beautiful suits!*

"Sir, if you do not mind me saying so, you look thinner today," notices my butler astutely.

"Oh, drat," I say. "My metabolism must be using up all of my calories just to maintain my height. Well, at least these suits will hang nicely off of my smooth, muscular body."

"Yes, sir. Quite."

I grab a navy blue pin-striped suit and throw another green suit with a dollar-bill pattern on it in my briefcase. I tie my tie—only once—no double Windsor knot for me. There's no chance a tall guy like me will trip over my tie!

I go downstairs and into the kitchen. I take a candy bar from on top of the refrigerator and put it in my pocket. One nice thing about being tall is that I can hide chocolate from my kids and extremely short wife. One bad thing is that I am worse at the limbo.

"Oh, sir, before I forget—you have some mail," says my butler.

I look at the mail. Just as I thought. More money. People are constantly sending me presents of money so that I will donate my sperm to them. This is because of my very good genes.

My Rolex watch tells me that it is late! I run out the door, wishing my fifty other butlers a good day.

Driving is easy for me because I am tall enough to steer and reach the gas pedal at the same time. Still, I invented a robot to push the brake pedal for me, not because I can't reach but because I'm lazy. And I'm pretty smart about stuff like robots.

I pop in a CD. I still use CDs because even the biggest iPod is too mini for my large fingers to navigate. I skip right to the secret track and listen to that first. (I always know if there is a secret track because my tall friends have already listened to the CD and they tell me ASAP.)

At work, I get into a debate and win. Height was certainly an advantage. I walk around the cubicles, peering over the tops of them and commanding respect. Sometimes, I slowly duck down as I walk around the cubicles so it looks like I am slowly melting. This is one of the many ways in which I am a good boss.

I stop by the bank during my lunch break and because I am tall, everyone calls me "sir" and gives me a deposit slip, instead of asking me where my mommy is and handing me a lollipop.

Back at work I go into some Internet chat rooms because I have some very important opinions about reality TV show contestants and I think it is helpful to others to read my views. In Internet chat rooms I never have to lie about my height. But I still do anyway, just to be droll.

Right before I go home I get a phone call—it's from a movie producer. They are making a film version of Curious George *and they want me to play the Man in the Yellow Hat. A dream come true! I'm glad I don't have to play the monkey...like some people would have to.*

Of course, because I can't be positive that that's what being tall would be like, I offer this alternative version of tallhood:

I wake up, my feet hanging over the bed like a maniac. It takes me fifteen minutes to find the light switch because I can barely see as far as my arm can reach. Damn it. 6:30 A.M. Time for my run.

When I go running, I am able to take half as many strides because my legs are twice as long, so thus I am twice as fat, unless I run twice as far, meaning I have to sleep twice as much, leaving me with half as many hours left in the day for my stretching. In this way I live out my existence.

A Neat Little Package

Well, folks, it seems as though we must say our good-byes. I feel as though our time together has been short, and yet we've had such a tall order to fill! Remember that shortness is a quality you share with many of the greatest artists, thinkers, and leaders of all time, but that it comes at a price. Remember that when you experience hard times because of people's prejudices, you are bigger than they are. Remember that if someone calls you short, *it's a compliment*. Also remember my advice about staying hydrated and not marrying chimpanzees. I'm gonna miss you guys.

Sometimes it may seem as if being tall would be the best thing in the world, but that is silly. Obviously being able to fly would be the best thing in the world, with singing underwater a close second. Think rationally, folks. I hope that is the one thing you come away with.

The big question is, if being tall is so great, why would almost everyone in the world consider him- or herself "short"? Could *almost everyone* be wrong about something? Impossible.

You can't really do much of anything about your height, so stop worrying about it. In a thousand years, people won't even have height—we will have discovered so many dimensions that humans will be measured in light-years and dark matter. But as long as we're all living on the same planet, remember that shortness has made the world what it is today: a sort of okay place with pretty good ice-cream flavors.

Bibliography

OTHER BOOKS ABOUT SHORTNESS

The Shortest Dog: Words and Wisdom from the World's Shortest Dog
The Shortest Cat: A Parody of the Shortest Dog, by Sir Paul McCartney
Short in America
Short in France
Short in Germany
Average Height in the United States of Mexico
Why Do My Pants Seem So Long?
Help Me Reach That
Get Me Out of This Boat: Fifty Short People Are Placed in a Lifeboat in the Middle of the Ocean. Who Will Survive?
I Didn't Agree to This: Experiments Done on Short People by Their Pets
Life Through the Cat Door: A Short Person's Ingenious Solution to the Mysteries of Life
Shortsightedness: An Ophthalmologist Commits Hundreds of Murders by Accident
A Review of "Shortsightedness": A Book Reviewer Accidentally Murders an Eye Doctor
Short Arms, Short Legs, No Head
The Last of the Giants: A Hip-Hop Version of the Bible

OTHER BOOKS BY THIS AUTHOR

Lost in the Ukraine: Help Me If You Are Reading This!
Girls Night Out: A Complete History of the Prison System in the Ukraine
The Last of the Mojitos

COMING SOON

The Elephant's Tears

Bibliography (NOT KIDDING THIS TIME...)

Anecdotage.com, http://www.anecdotage.com.

Anne Case and Christina Paxson, "Stature and Status: Height, Ability, and Labor Market Outcomes: Working Paper 12466," (Cambridge, MA: National Bureau of Economic Research, 2006).

Bean, R. Bennett, "Stature throughout the World," Science 67, no. 1723 (1928): 1-5.

Bryant J., E. Loveman, D. Chase, B. Mihaylova, C. Cave, K. Gerard, and R. Milne, "Clinical effectiveness and cost-effectiveness of growth hormone in adults in relation to impact on quality of life: a systematic review and economic evaluation," Health Technology Assessment 6, no. 19 (2000).

CBS News Online, "Forget Napoleon – Height Rules: Study Finds Each Inch Could Mean an Extra $800 a Year," http://www.cbsnews.com/stories/2003/10/17/health/main578654.shtml.

Celebheights.com, http://www.celebheights.com/.

Clean Funny Joke, "You are so short..." http://www.cleanfunnyjoke.com/index.php?b=23&t=290&start=0.

Cline, M.G., K.E. Meredith, J.T. Boyer, and B. Burrows, "Decline of height with age in adults in a general population sample: estimating maximum height and distinguishing birth cohort effects from actual loss of stature with aging," Human Biology 61, no. 3 (1989): 415-25.

Consumeraffairs.com, "Dating Sites Short on Truth: Users Most Likely to Exaggerate their Height," http://www.consumeraffairs.com/news04/2007/02/valentine_dating_sites.html.

Glenday, Craig, Guiness World Records 2007, (London: Guinness World Records Ltd., 2006).

Harper, Barry, "Beauty, Stature and the Labour Market: A British Cohort Study," (study, London Guidhall University, 1999), http://www.essex.ac.uk/ilr/eeeg/Conference1/Harper.pdf.

Hershey, Bodin, It's a Small World, (New York: Cowad-McCann Inc., 1934).

Hy Roth and Robert Cromie, The Little People, (New York: Everest House, 1980).

The Internet Movie Database, http://imdb.com/.

Keogh, Frank, "Knight's crowning glory," BBC Sport, June 2, 2003, http://news.bbc.co.uk/sport1/hi/other_sports/horse_racing/2941894.stm.

Kahn, Joseph, "Chinese People's Republic Is Unfair to Its Short People," The New York Times, May 21, 2004, http://query.nytimes.com/gst/fullpage.html?sec=health&res=990CE1DA113FF932A15756C0A9629C8B63.

Komlos, John, "The Anthropometric History of Early-Modern France," European Review of Economic History 7, no. 02 (2003): 159-189.
"Shrinking in a Growing Economy? The Mystery of Physical Stature During the Industrial Revolution," The Journal of Economic History 58, no. 3 (1998): 779-802.

Krajewska, Barbara, "Arsenic and the Emperor," Napoleon.org, http://www. napoleon. org/en/reading_room/articles/files/arsenic_emperor.asp.

Kralic, Adam, "Attila the Hun: Major political events and the death of Attila the Hun," posting to About.com, http://ancienthistory.about.com/cs/attilathehun/a/attilathehun.htm.

Mayell, Hillary, "Hobbit-Like Human Ancestor Found in Asia," National Geographic News, October 27, 2004, http://news.nationalgeographic.com/news/2004/10/1027_041027_homo_floresiensis_2.html.

Medical News Today, "Cost for Growth Hormone Therapy Doesn't Measure Up," http://www.medicalnewstoday.com/medicalnews.php?newsid=39377.

MSNBC Online, "The world's smallest car: Wheels made up of just 60 atoms each," http://www.msnbc.msn.com/id/9778004/.

Niewenweg, R., M.L. Smit, M.J.E. Waienkamp, and J.M. Wit, "Adult height corrected for shrinking and secular trend," Annals of Human Biology 30, no. 5 (2003): 563-569.

NME, "Man shot over James Brown's height: Argument over the late Godfather of Soul ends in gunfire," January 11, 2007, http://www.nme.com/news/james-brown/25768.

Oidemizu, Takayuki, "The Quest for the Perfect Racket: Advances in Tennis Racket Design," Illumin, December 6, 2006, http://illumin.usc.edu/article.php?articleID=68&page=4.

Parker, Gretchen, "Limb lengthening tests human willpower: Patients endure unimaginable pain for a few inches," Associated Press, February 18, 2004, http://www.msnbc.msn.com/id/4242093/#storyContinued.

Reitman, Valerie, "We clicked: Matchmaking tools, including psychological tests and personality profiles, are helping online daters narrow their search for 'the one,'" The Los Angeles Times, April 26, 2004, http://www.eharmony.com/singles/servlet/press/articles?id=15.

Richard H. Steckel and Joseph M. Prince, "Tallest in the World: Native Americans of the Great Plains in the Nineteenth Century," American Economic Review 91, no. 1 (2001): 287-294.

Rieser, Patricia A., Growth Hormone Deficiency, (Glen Head, NY: Human Growth Foundation, Inc., 1979), http://www.hgfound.org/growth.html.

Romaine, Mertie E., General Tom Thumb and His Lady, (Taunton, MA: William S. Sullwood Publishing Inc., 1976).

Short Persons Support, http://www.shortsupport.org/.

Sun, Lena H., "Metrorail Car's Trial Run Lets Short Riders Get a Grip," The Washington Post, February 8, 2007, http://www.washingtonpost.com/wp-dyn/content/article/2007/02/07/AR2007020702505.html.

The Times of India, "World's smallest temple discovered in China," November 2, 2005, http://timesofindia.indiatimes.com/articleshow/msid-1282270,curpg-1.cms.

Watts, Jonathan, "A tall order," The Guardian, December 15, 2003, http://www.guardian.co.uk/china/story/0,7369,1107283,00.html#article_continue.

Wikipedia, http://en.wikipedia.org/wiki/Main_Page.

INDEX

Abbott, Bud, 96
achondroplasia, 20
actors and actresses, 87-97, 98-100, 128-129; action, 97; child, 135; comedy, 96; movie, 87-94; television, 95
Adams, John, 108
Adler, Alfred, 78
Ahmadinejad, Mahmoud, 112
Akers, Carrie, 33
Alexander, Jason, 95
Alexander the Great, 81-82
Allen, Woody, 126
amusement park rides, 47
anacondas, 39
Andretti, Mario, 105
anthropometry, 27
Antommarchi, Francesco, 79
artists, 119
Astin, Sean, 89, 163
astronauts, 118
athletes, 101-109; baseball, 102, 103; basketball, 101; boxing, 106; bullfighting, 105; figure skating, 105; football, 104; gymnastics, 136; horseracing, 135; marathon running, 102, 104; car racing, 105; sharp shooting, 106; soccer, 104; speed skating, 106; tennis, 1-4-105; weightlifting, 105
Atienzar, Maribel, 105
Attila the Hun, 82-83
authors, 124-125
auxology, 18
Babyface, 133
Bacon, Kevin, 92
Balzac, Honoré de, 124
Banderas, Antonio, 126
Barnum, P. T., 34-36
Barty, Billy, 132
Basua tribe, 24
bears, 33, 39
Beethoven, Ludwig van, 120
Ben-Gurion, David, 111

Benatar, Pat, 121
Benigni, Roberto, 92
Berlusconi, Silvio, 112
Bernal, Gael Garcia, 128
Berry, Halle, 94
Bes (god), 156
birds, 40
Black, Debbie, 101
Black, Jack, 91
Bogart, Humphrey, 98
Bogues, Tyrone "Muggsy," 101
Bonaduce, Danny, 95
Bonaparte, Napoleon, 78, 80-81, 112
Boxer, Barbara, 112
Boykins, Earl, 101
Breger, da Silva, Douglas Maistre, 33
Bronte, Charlotte, 125
Brooks, David James, Jr., 122
Brooks, Mel, 126
Brown, James, 122
Buell, Jed, 100
Bump, Mary Lavinia Warren, 35-36
Bush, George H. W., 110
Bush, George W., 110
business and economics, 54-56
businessmen, 113
camera angles, 99
Carnegie, Andrew, 113
cars, 43, 164
Carter, Jimmy, 110
Carter, Nell, 95
Case, Anne, 55
cats, 40
Chan, Jackie, 97
Chang, Michael, 164
chimpanzees, 38
Churchill, Winston, 111
circuses, 34-37
Clinton, William J., 110
clothes, 165
Coleman, Gary, 135
Collins, Phil, 121
Comaneci, Nadia, 136
comedy teams, 96
confidence, social, 55, 143-144
Conner, Bart, 136
constitutional growth delay (CGD), 20
Copeland, Lil' Zane, 133

coping, 166
Costello, Lou, 96
coxswains, 134
Crawford, Joan, 129
criminals, 114-116
Cruise, Tom, 88
Cruz, Penelope, 92
Currie, Nancy, 118
Daniel, Jack, 113
Darin, Bobby, 98
Davis, Sammy, Jr., 120
Davis, Warwick, 89
Dean, James, 92
Dench, Judi, 94
DeVito, Danny, 67
Dewey, Thomas E., 110
Dickens, Little Jimmy, 120-121
Dinka Nilotles tribes, 24
Dinklage, Peter, 88
directors, 126
ditches, 99
Dole, Robert, 110
Downey, Robert, Jr., 92
Dr. Ruth, 127
Driver, Minnie, 99
Dukakis, Michael, 109, 110
Dupri, Jermaine, 133
dwarfism, 20, 34, 36
dwarfs, 88, 89, 132; proportionate, 34-37, 100, 103; and royalty, 36-37
Dylan, Bob, 121
eeyeekalduks, 76
Efe tribe, 24
Eisenhower, Dwight D., 110
Electra, Carmen, 95
elephants, 39
Ellison, Harlan, 125
elves, 75, 76
Eskimos, 24
Estevez, Emilio, 92
eye contact, 140
fairy tales, 74-77
Falk, Peter, 90
Faulkner, William, 125
Field, Sally, 93
Fine, Larry, 96
fish, 40
Fitzgerald, F. Scott, 125
Flores (island), 28-29
Ford, Gerald, R., 110
Fox, Michael J., 88, 98, 149

Fromme, Lynette "Squeaky," 115
Fuller, Buckminster, 127
Gaedel, Eddie, 103
Gagarin, Yuri, 118
Gandhi, Mohandas, 112
Garland, Judy, 93
Garofalo, Janeane, 90
genetics, 18
Getty, Estelle, 95
gnomes, 76
Goldwater, Barry, 110
Gordon, Jeff, 105
Gore, Albert, 110
Gottfried, Gilbert, 88
gravity, 25
Grissom, Gus, 118
growth, human, 18-20, 30
growth hormone (GH), 20, 161-162
Gulley, Jr., Dan, 122
gunners, turret ball, 134
Hamill, Mark, 129
Hamilton, Scott, 105
Hancock, John, 112
Hardy, Oliver, 96
Hawking, Stephen, 134
Hayek, Salma, 91
height, 23-25, 26-29; by gender, 25; historically, 26-29; by populations, 23-24, 27; by race, 25; by time of day, 25
heightism, 46-47, 54-56
Hinduism, 155
Hirohito, Emperor, 111
Hoffman, Dustin, 93
Homo florienses, 28-29
Hoskins, Bob, 89
Houdini, Harry, 96
Howard, Jerome "Curly," 96
Howard, Moe, 96
Hudson, Jeffrey, 36
human growth hormone (HGH), 162
hummingbirds, 40
Humphrey, Hubert H., 110
Hunt, Linda, 94
Hunter, Holly, 94

idiopathic short stature, 20
Il, Kim Jong, 112
Industrial Revolution, 27
insects, 39-40
insults. See jokes and insults.
intelligence, 55
intolerance, 71
irony, 71
Jameson, Jenna, 91
Jeremy, Ron, 92
Joan of Arc, Saint, 157
jobs. See work and jobs.
jockeys, 135
Jones, Kimberly "L'il Kim," 133
Johnson, Lyndon, 110
Johnson, Temeka, 101
jokes and insults, 48-49, 72-73, 64-66
Kant, Immanuel, 123
Keaton, Buster, 96
Keats, John, 125
Keeler, "Wee Willie," 102
kelp, 40
Kennedy, John F., 110
Kerry, John, 110
"kid" syndrome, 141
King, Billie Jean, 104
kobolds, 75
kurupiras, 76
Ladd, Alan, 100
Laurel, Stan, 96
Lawrence, Martin, 92
Lee, Bruce, 97
Lee, Spike, 126
leg lengthening, 158-160
leprechauns, 75
leptons, 42
leszy, 76
Lewis, Emmanuel, 135
Lewis, Shari, 129
Li, Jet, 97
Lincoln, Abraham, 99, 109
lingerie, 164
Liu, Lucy, 91
Lohan, Lindsay, 91
Loroupe, Tegla, 104
Lorre, Peter, 88, 126
Lucci, Susan, 95
Madison, James, 108
Magri, Count, 36
Mahler, Gustav, 121
Manson, Charles, 115
Maranville, "Rabbit," 102
Marx, Chico, 96
Marx, Harpo, 96
Matina, Bela, 33

Matina, Lajos, 33
Matina, Maltjus, 33
Mauna Kea, 42
McGovern, George, 110
Mead, Margaret, 127
media, 64-67, 77
Meredith, Burgess, 91
Midler, Bette, 91, 128
Mitchell, Margaret, 125
Miyake, Yoshinobu, 105
Mondale, Walter F., 110
monkeys, 38
Monroe, Marilyn, 90
Moore, Julianne, 90
Morita, Noriyuki "Pat," 91
Mount Everest, 42
mountains, 42
movies, tricks of, 98-100
Muhammed, Gul, 32
musicians, 120-122
Myers, Mike, 90
mythological creatures, 74-77
Napoleon complex, 78
natural selection, 51-53
Nelson, George "Baby Face," 114
Nelson, Horatio, 127
Netherlands, 25
Newman, Randy, 70-71
nicknames, 48-50
Nixon, Richard M., 110
North Korea, 25
nutrition, 23, 25, 27
O'Donnell, Chris, 99
O'Neal, Shaquille, 50
Oakley, Annie, 106
Onassis, Aristotle, 113
organisms, 39
Oscars, 92-94
Osment, Haley Joel, 89
osteoporosis, 31
ostriches, 40
Pacino, Al, 94
parasites, 38-39
Parker, Bonnie, 114
Parker, Sarah Jessica, 89-90
Parra, Derek, 106
Parton, Dolly, 121
Patek, Freddie, 102
Paxson, Christina, 55
Pelé, 104
Pereira Rocha, Claudia, 33

Perot, Ross, 113
Phife Dawg, 133
philosophers, 123
Picasso, Pablo, 119
Pickford, Mary, 93
Pitt, Brad, 98
Plains Indians, 27
plants, 40
poems, 42-43
politicians, 107-112; and television, 109, 110
Portman, Natalie, 88
presidents, 108-110
Prince, 120
puberty, 20, 30, 54
pygmies, 28
quarks, 42
Reagan, Ronald, 110
Ricci, Christina, 128
Richards, Gordon, Sir, 135
Richebourg, 116
Riggs, Bobby, 104
Rochus, Oliver, 104-105
Rodin, Auguste, 119
Roman Empire, 36-37
Rooney, Mickey, 93
Roosevelt, Franklin Delano, 111
Rudy (movie), 89
Sanders, Barry, 104
Schwarzenegger, Arnold, 67, 97
Scorsese, Martin, 126
seahorses, 40
Selassie, Haile, 156
sharks, 40
Sheen, Charlie, 92
Sheen, Martin, 92
Shoemaker, Willie, 135
shoes, elevator, 98, 112
Short People (song), 71
Short, Martin, 88
Shrek (movie), 77
shrinkage, human, 31
Simmons, Richard, 127
Simon, Paul, 121
singers, hip-hop, 133
Sisqo, 133
size records, animals, 38-40; couples, 33; human height, 32-33; men, 32; non-living, 42; plants, 40; twins, 33; women, 32
Smith, Joseph, 156
snakes, 39
somatotropin. See growth hormone (GH).

Spade, David, 90
Stalin, Joseph, 111
Stallone, Sylvester, 97
Stein, Ben, 92
steroids, anabolic, 162
Stevenson, Adlai, 110
Stowe, Harriet, Beecher, 124
Stratton, Charles Sherwood. See Thumb, Tom.
Stravinsky, Igor, 121
stretching, 163
subway handlebars, 165
Süleymanoglu, Naim, 105
Taft, William, 109
Taipei 101
Taiwan, 43
Taylor, Elizabeth, 93
Temple, Shirley, 88
temples, Buddhist, 157
Teresa, Mother, 105
Terror of Tiny Town, The (movie), 100
Three Stooges, 96
Thugwane, Josia, 104
Thumb, Tom, 34-36
Tober, Runi, 115-116
Tolkien, J. R. R., 75
Toulouse-Lautrec, Henri de, 119
Troyer, Verne, 88
Truman, Harry S, 110
Tubman, Harriet, 127
Twins (movie), 67
Van Buren, Martin, 108
Van Dyck, Anthony, 37
Veeck, Bill, 103
Victoria, Queen, 112
Voltaire, 123
Walcott, Joe, 106
Walker, Nancy, 95
Washington, George, 108
Wayne, John, 99
weather, 24
Webb, Spudd, 101
West, Mae, 91
whales, 40
Whistler, James Abbott McNeil, 119
Wilder, Laura Ingalls, 125
Winkler, Henry, 129
Wood, Elijah, 89
work and jobs, 54-56
World War II, 111
Yorke, Thom, 121
Zarate, Lucia, 32